Knit Socks
For All Seasons

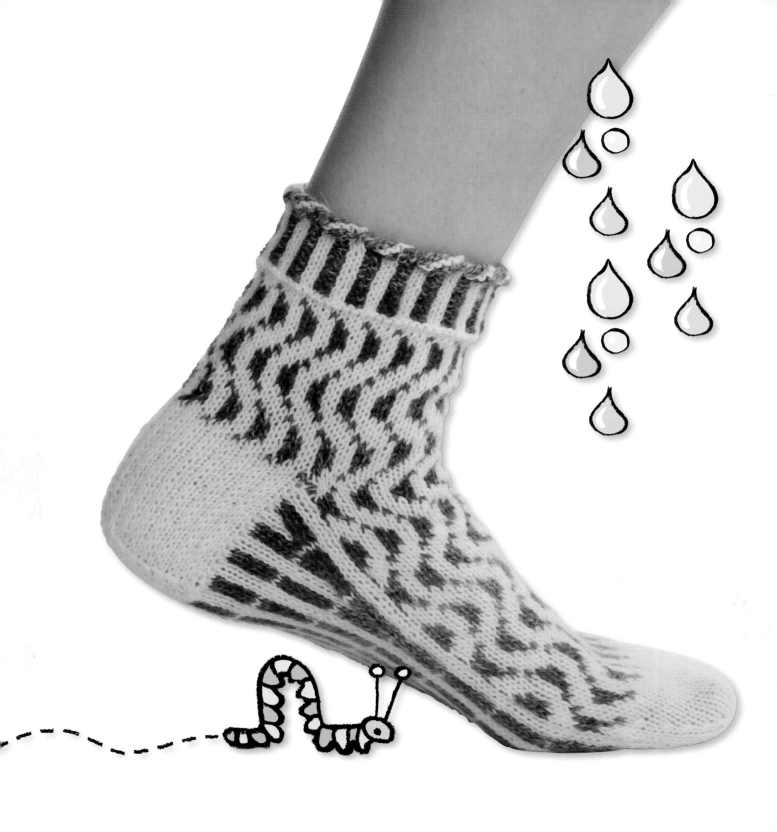

Stephanie van der Linden

Knit Socks For All Seasons

TRAFALGAR SQUARE
North Pomfret, Vermont

First published in the United States of America in 2012 by
Trafalgar Square Books
North Pomfret, Vermont 05053
www.trafalgarbooks.com

Originally published in German as *Socken rund ums Jahr*

This edition is published by arrangement with Claudia Böhme Rights & Literary Agency, Hannover, Germany (www.agency.boehme.com)

ISBN: 978-1-57076-526-1

Library of Congress Control Number: 2011942243

PROJECT MANAGEMENT: Eva-Barbara Hentschel
ILLUSTRATIONS: Ursula Schwab, Handewitt
TEXT: Britta John
PHOTOS: Frechverlag LLC; lighting Michael Ruder, Stuttgart
LAYOUT: Petra Theilfarth
TRANSLATION FROM GERMAN: C. Elizabeth Wellenstein & Carol Huebscher Rhoades

We wish to thank the companies Coats, Coats LLC, Kenzingen, www.coatsgmbh.de and Zitron, Wickede (Ruhr), www.atelierzitron.de for the support of this book.

Printed in China

10 9 8 4 6 5 4 3 2 1

Knit Socks For All Seasons

Spring, summer, fall and winter — each season has its own unique colors, shapes and textures. If you move through the seasons with open eyes, you'll notice Mother Nature's little works of art everywhere you go.

I have translated my impressions of nature into new sock ideas for you to enjoy. The result is a large variety of pattern and shapes that I have collected here in this book for you. I guarantee, there is something here for everyone!

You'll find detailed material lists, easy to understand instructions, well-charted patterns, and a comprehensive glossary of basic techniques.

I wish you great pleasure in knitting socks for all seasons.

Stephanie van der Linden

8 Fantastically Soft

Long before you see any signs of spring, new socks can be sprouting from the needles. As a tribute to those early crocus buds, this delicate lace pattern in a white silk/wool blend symbolizes the hopeful beginning of a new season.

Fantastically Soft

LEVEL OF DIFFICULTY
Experienced

SIZES
Women's: U.S. 5-6, 6-7, 7-8, 8-9, 9-10, 10-11, 11-12 (European 36, 37, 38, 39, 40, 41, 42)

Leg circumference: 8 ¼-10 ¾ in (21-27 cm)

Foot circumference: 8-9 ¾ in (20-25 cm)

The length of the sock can be determined by using the respective shoe size.

MATERIALS
Yarn: Fingering (CYCA #1), Regia Silk 4-ply (55% wool/25% nylon/20% silk; 219 yd/50 g), Natural heather (#0002), 100 g

Needles: 2 circulars U.S. size 0 or 2.5 (2 or 3 mm) or size needed to obtain gauge

Crochet hook: U. S. size C-2 (2.5 or 3 mm)

Tapestry needle

GAUGE
30 sts and 42 rows in stockinette = 4 x 4 in (10 x 10 cm)

35 sts and 40 rows in instep pattern = 4 x 4 in (10 x 10 cm)

KNITTING BOOKLET
Charts, pp. 2-3

TECHNIQUES
Right- and left-leaning increases, p. 108

Toe-up construction on 2 circulars, p. 114

Short row Wrap and Turn (w&t), pp. 110-111

Stretchy bind-off, p. 118

Crocheted Picot edging, p. 115

PATTERNS FOR INSTEP AND LEG
See charts in Booklet, pp. 2-3

INSTRUCTIONS

TOE-UP CONSTRUCTION
With one circular, CO 13 sts and slide them to the cable. With second circular, pick up and knit sts from the purl ridge on the underside of the cast-on row.

Ndl 1: K12, drop 1 st.
Ndl 2: K12.
(12 sts on each ndl)

Inc rnd:
Ndls 1 and 2 (inc rnd worked the same way on each needle): K2, M1R, knit until 2 sts rem, M1L, k2.
Work 1 rnd in St st.
Repeat these 2 rnds three more times.
Work 1 inc rnd and then 2 rnds stockinette.
Repeat these three rnds 3 more times.
Work 1 inc rnd and then 3 rnds stockinette.
Repeat these 4 rnds once more.
(32 sts on each ndl)

TRANSITION TO INSTEP
At this point, you must determine the desired length of the foot. Work around in stockinette until piece measures 2 in (5 cm) less than total length.

INSTEP
Ndl 1: Work charted instep pattern.
Ndl 2: K32.
Continuing as set, working Rnds 1-50 in charted pattern over sts on ndl 1 and knitting the 32 sts on ndl 2. (71+32 sts)
Ndl 1: Work 51st rnd of instep pattern.

Shoe size: U.S. (Euro)	5-6 (36)	6-7 (37)	7-8 (38)	8-9 (39)	9-10 (40)	10-11 (41)	11-12 (42)
Foot length	9 ½ in	9 ½ in	9 ½-9 ¾ in	10 in	10 ¼ in	10 ½-10 ¾ in	10 ¾ in
	(23.5 cm)	(24 cm)	(24.5-25 cm)	(25.5 cm)	(26 cm)	(26.5-27 cm)	(27.5 cm)
Length of toe	2 ½ in	2 ¾ in	3 in	3 ¼ in	3 ½ in	3 ¾ in	4 in
	(6.5 cm)	(7 cm)	(8 cm)	(8.5 cm)	(9 cm)	(9.5 cm)	(10.5 cm)

HEEL

Shape an inverted heart heel by working back and forth across the 32 sts of ndl 2. Set sts on ndl 1 aside while you work heel:

Row 1: (RS): Knit to last 2 sts, w&t.

Row 2: (WS): Purl to last 2 sts, w&t.

Row 3: Knit until 2 sts before the last wrapped st, w&t.

Row 4: Purl until 2 sts before the last wrapped st, w&t.

Repeat rows 3 and 4 until there are 7 wrapped sts on each side of 4 unwrapped sts in the center.

Work the heel flap back and forth across the sts on ndl 2. Knit the last st of each row together with the next st on ndl 1 as follows:

Row 1 (RS): K4, *k1 wrapped st, k1, rep from * 5 more times, k1 wrapped st, sl 1 kwise, sl first st from ndl 1 kwise and knit these 2 sts tog (= ssk); turn.

Row 2: (WS) Sl 1, p17, p1 wrapped st, p1, rep from* 5 more times, p1 wrapped st, sl the last st pwise, sl the 1st st on ndl 1 pwise and purl these 2 sts tog; turn.

Row 3: Sl 1, k to within 1 st of end, ssk (see Row 1), turn.

Row 4: Sl 1, p to within 1 st of end, sl 2 as if to p, p2tog (see Row 2), turn.

Rep Rows 3 and 4 another 15 times.

(37+32 sts)

TRANSITION TO LEG PATTERN

Ndl 2: *K8, M1, rep from * 2 more times, k8, k1tbl, and p2 from ndl 1.

(34+38 sts)

Sl first 2 sts of ndl 2 onto ndl 1.

(36+36)

LEG

Ndl 1: Work 18 sts of leg pattern twice.

Ndl 2: Work as for ndl 1.

Work 48 rnds leg pattern (2 x Rnds 1-24).

CUFF

Ndl 1: Work 18 sts of Rnd 49 twice.

Ndl 2: Work as ndl 1.

Repeat Rnd 49 13 times more.

Bind off all sts loosely, moving last loop to crochet hook. Work the crocheted picot edging around top of each leg: *Ch 3, sl st into first st of chain, skip 2 sts on bind-off row, sc into next st; rep from * around.

Cut yarn, thread end onto tapestry needle, and pull end through last st.

FINISHING

Cut yarn and weave in ends neatly on WS.

Make the second sock the same way.

Fresh and Quick

Celebrate the season! Like the colorful ribbons of a Maypole on the green, the tweed yarn contains little flecks of color throughout. Your feet will love the soft feel of this wool blend yarn.

Fresh and Quick

LEVEL OF DIFFICULTY
Easy

SIZES
Women's: U.S. 5-6, 6-7, 7-8, 8-9, 9-10, 10-11, 11-12 (European 36, 37, 38, 39, 40, 41, 42)

Leg circumference: 8 ¼-9 ¾ in (21-25 cm)

Foot circumference: 8-8 ¾ in (20-22 cm)

The length of the sock can be determined by using the respective shoe size.

MATERIALS
Yarn: Fingering (CYCA #1), Trekking Tweed (75% wool/25% nylon; 462 yd/100g), Light sage, (#285), 100 g

Needles: set of 5 dpn or 2 circulars U.S. size 0 or 2.5 (2 or 3 mm) or size needed to obtain gauge

Cable needle

Tapestry needle

GAUGE
32 sts and 40 rows in stockinette = 4 x 4 in (10 x 10 cm)

33 sts and 40 rows in heel pattern = 4 x 4 in (10 x 10 cm)

KNITTING BOOKLET
Chart, p. 3

TECHNIQUES
Make 1 (M1) increase, p. 108

Right- and left-leaning decreases, p. 109

The "gap" on heel turn, p. 111

PATTERNS FOR LEG, HEEL AND FOOT
See charts in Booklet, p. 3.

INSTRUCTIONS

CO 64 sts and divide sts evenly onto 4 dpn, with 16 on each ndl. Join to knit in the round, being careful not to twist the cast-on row.

Work 72 rnds in leg pattern (4 x Rnds 1-16 and then 1 x Rnds 1-8)

Slip the last st (unworked) of the last rnd from ndl 4 to ndl 1

(17+16+16+15 sts)

Move sts on ndls 3 and 4 onto one dpn and work heel flap. Inc with M1 between ndls 1 and 4; turn. Set-up row: K4, *p1, k3; rep from * 6 more times, M1 between ndls 3 and 2; turn. (33 heel sts)

Work 32 rows following heel flap chart. Cross cables on RS rows.

Turn the heel:
Row 1 (RS): K18, ssk, k1; turn.
Row 2 (WS): Sl 1 pwise, p4, p2tog, p1; turn.
Row 3: Sl 1 pwise, knit until 1 st before the gap, ssk, k1; turn.
Row 4: Sl 1 pwise, purl until 1 st before the gap, p2tog, p1; turn.
Rep rows 3 and 4 five more times, until 19 heel sts rem.

GUSSET

Ndl 4: K19 heel sts, pick up and knit 16 new sts along side of heel flap.

Ndls 1 and 2: Work 33 sts in foot pattern.

Ndl 3: Pick up and knit 16 new sts along side of heel flap, k8 sts from Ndl 4, k2tog.

Ndl 4: K25

(17+16+25+25 sts)

Rnds 1 and 2:

Ndls1 and 2: Work 33 sts in charted foot pattern.

Ndls 3 and 4: Knit.

Rnd 3:

Ndls 1 and 2: Work 33 sts in foot pattern.

Ndl 3: K1, ssk, knit to end.

Ndl 4: Knit to last 3 sts, k2tog, k1.

Repeat Rnds 1-3 eight times.

(17+16+16+16 sts)

Ndls 1 and 2: Work 33 sts in foot pattern.

Ndls3 and 4: Knit.

Continue working in pattern until foot is 2 in (5 cm) less than desired total length (see Table).

BAND TOE

Ndl 1: K2tog, knit rem sts in round.

(16+16+16+16 sts)

Decrease Round:

Ndl 1: K1, ssk, knit to end.

Ndl 2: Knit to last three sts, k2tog, k1.

Ndl 3: Work as for ndl 1.

Ndl 4: Work as for ndl 2.

Continue around in stockinette, decreasing as follows:

Knit 3 rnds and decrease on Rnd 4.

(Knit 2 rnds and dec on Rnd 3) 2 times.

(Knit 1 rnd and dec on Rnd 2) 4 times.

Decrease on each of the next 6 rnds.

FINISHING

Cut yarn, thread end on tapestry needle, and pull strand through rem 8 sts.

Weave in ends neatly on WS.

Make second sock the same way.

Shoe size: U.S. (Euro)	5-6 (36)	6-7 (37)	7-8 (38)	8-9 (39)	9-10 (40)	10-11 (41)	11-12 (42)
Foot length	9 ½ in	9 ½ in	9 ½-9 ¾ in	10 in	10 ¼ in	10 ½-10 ¾ in	10 ¾ in
	(23.5 cm)	(24 cm)	(24.5-25 cm)	(25.5 cm)	(26 cm)	(26.5-27 cm)	(27.5 cm)
Sock length heel to toe	7 ¼ in	7 ½ in	7 ¾-8 in	8 in	8 ¼ in in	8 ½-8 ¾ in	8 ¾ in
	(18.5 cm)	(19 cm)	(19.5-20 cm)	(20.5 cm)	(21 cm)	(21.5-22 cm)	(22.5 cm)

Nicely Structured

Everything outside is waking up. Like busy bees, the pattern of this sock moves through the heather grey yarn, a subtle contrast to the colors of Spring.

Nicely Structured

LEVEL OF DIFFICULTY
Intermediate

SIZES
Women's: U.S. 5-6, 6-7, 7-8, 8-9, 9-10, 10-11, 11-12 (European 36, 37, 38, 39, 40, 41, 42)

Leg circumference: 8 ¼-10 ¾ in (21-27 cm)

Foot circumference: 8-9 ¾ in (20-25 cm)

The length of the sock can be determined by using the respective shoe size.

MATERIALS
Yarn: Fingering (CYCA #1), Regia 4-ply (75% wool, 25% nylon; 229 yd/50 g), Light gray heather (#1991), 100 g

Needles: 2 circulars U.S. size 0 or 1.5 (2 or 2.5 mm) or size needed to obtain gauge

2 stitch markers

Tapestry needle

GAUGE
32 sts and 40 rows in stockinette = 4 x 4 in (10 x 10 cm)

KNITTING BOOKLET
Chart, p. 4

TECHNIQUES
Make 1 (M1) increase, p. 108

The "gap" on heel turn, p. 111

INSTEP
See chart in Booklet, p. 4.

INSTRUCTIONS

CO 64 sts on one circular and knit 1 row. On the next row, knit the first 32 sts with circular ndl 1 and the last 32 sts with circular ndl 2; join to work in the round, being careful not to twist the cast-on row.

Rnd 1
Ndl 1: *K1tbl, p1*; rep from * to * 15 times.
Ndl 2: Work as for Ndl 1.

Repeat Rnd 1 14 times = 15 rnds total.

Knit 1 rnd, purl 1 rnd, knit 1 rnd. On the last rnd, increase 1 st at the end of each ndl with M1. (33+33 sts)

LEG
Ndl 1: Work 33 sts in leg pattern (3 repeats around).
Ndl 2: Work as for ndl 1.

Work 45 rnds in pattern following chart in booklet (2 x Rnds 1-18 and then 1 x Rnds 1-9).

HEEL
When the leg is 6 ¼ in (16 cm) long, begin the heel shaping. Work all increases with M1.

Rnd 1:
Ndl 1: Work 11 sts in pattern (Rnd 1 of leg pattern), M1, place marker, M1, 11 sts in pattern, M1, place marker, M1, 11 sts in pattern.
Ndl 2: Work 33 sts in pattern (Rnd 1 of leg pattern) following chart (3 x 11 sts).

Rnds 2 and 3:
Ndl 1: Work 11 sts in pattern (Rnd 2), k1, slip marker, p1, work 11 sts in pattern, k1, slip marker, p1, 11 sts in pattern.
Ndl 2: Work 33 sts in pattern (Rnd 2 of leg pattern) following chart.
(37+33 sts)

Rnd 4:
Ndl 1: Work 11 sts in pattern, knit to 1 st before marker, M1, k1, slip marker, p1, 11 sts in pattern, k1, M1, knit to 2nd marker, slip marker, p1, 11 sts in pattern.
Ndl 2: Work 33 sts in pattern following chart.

Rnds 5 and 6:
Ndl 1: Work 11 sts in pattern, knit to marker, slip marker, p1, 11 sts in pattern, knit to marker, slip marker, p1, 11 sts in pattern.
Ndl 2: Work 33 sts in pattern (Rnd 2 of leg pattern) following chart.

Repeat Rnds 4-6 another 12 times. There should now be 14 knit sts on each side of the central pattern repeat (Rnd 6 of pattern). (63+33 sts)

The heel is turned by working short rows back and forth over the sts on ndl 1:
Row 1 (RS): K32, ssk, k1; turn.
Row 2 (WS): Sl 1 purlwise, p2, p2tog, p1; turn.
Row 3: Knit to 1 st before the gap, ssk, k2; turn.
Row 4: Purl to 1 st before the gap, p2tog, p1; turn.

Repeat Rows 3-4 another 13 times. (33+33 sts)

FOOT

Ndl 1: K32, p1.
Ndl 2: K33 following charted pattern (beginning on Rnd 11).

Continue as set with stockinette on sole and pattern on instep until foot is 2 in (5 cm) less than total foot length (see Table).

BAND TOE

Knit 1 rnd.

Shaping:
Ndl 1: K1, ssk, knit until 3 sts remain on needle and end with k2tog, k1.
Ndl 2: Work as for Ndl 1.

Continue around in stockinette, decreasing as follows:
Knit 3 rnds and decrease on Rnd 4.
(Knit 2 rnds and dec on Rnd 3) 2 times.
(Knit 1 rnd and dec on Rnd 2) 4 times.
Decrease on each of the next 6 rnds.

FINISHING

Cut yarn and thread end onto tapestry needle. Pull end through remaining 8 (10) sts. Pull tight and then weave in all ends neatly on WS.

Make the second sock the same way.

Knit and purl texture patterns should always be knit at a slightly tighter gauge than expected. You might want to change to needles one U.S. size (.25-.5 mm) smaller than the size given in the pattern. If the knit-purl pattern is worked loosely on the leg and foot, the purl stitches will have less visual effect and the pattern will look fuzzy and unclear. The more switching between knit and purl, the more tightly knit the sock should be. The larger the stockinette areas in the texture pattern are, the more similar the gauge will be to stockinette or reverse stockinette.

Shoe size: U.S. (Euro)	5-6 (36)	6-7 (37)	7-8 (38)	8-9 (39)	9-10 (40)	10-11 (41)	11-12 (42)
Foot length	9 ½ in	9 ½ in	9 ½-9 ¾ in	10 in	10 ¼ in	10 ½-10 ¾ in	10 ¾ in
	(23.5 cm)	(24 cm)	(24.5-25 cm)	(25.5 cm)	(26 cm)	(26.5-27 cm)	(27.5 cm)
Sock length heel to toe	7 ¼ in	7 ½ in	7 ¾-8 in	8 in	8 ¼ in in	8 ½-8 ¾ in	8 ¾ in
	(18.5 cm)	(19 cm)	(19.5-20 cm)	(20.5 cm)	(21 cm)	(21.5-22 cm)	(22.5 cm)

Blooming Gorgeous

Light orange is a perfect color for spring: a beautifully entwined cuff that appears like a calyx is the perfect addition to the pattern. The bamboo yarn provides the utmost in wearable comfort, even when worn in the heat of summer.

Blooming Gorgeous

LEVEL OF DIFFICULTY
Intermediate

SIZES
Women's: U.S. 5-6, 6-7, 7-8, 8-9, 9-10, 10-11, 11-12 (European 36, 37, 38, 39, 40, 41, 42)

Leg circumference: 8 ¼-10 ¾ in (21-27 cm)

Foot circumference: 8-9 ¾ in (20-25 cm)

Men's: U.S. 8 ½, 9, 10 ½, 11 ½ (European 42, 43, 44, 45)

Leg circumference: 9 ½-11 ½ in (24-29 cm)

Foot circumference: 9-11 in (23-28 cm)

The length of the sock can be determined by using the respective shoe size.

Instructions and stitch counts in parentheses or following a slash refer to Men's sizes.

MATERIALS
Yarn: Fingering (CYCA #1), Trekking Pro Natura (75% wool/25% bamboo; 459 yd/100 g), Orange (#1513), 100 g

Needles: 2 circulars or set of 5 dpn U.S. size 0 or 1.5 (2 or 2.5 mm) or size needed to obtain gauge

Cable needle

Tapestry needle

GAUGE
32 sts and 42 rows in stockinette = 4 x 4 in (10 x 10 cm)

KNITTING BOOKLET
Charts, p. 5

TECHNIQUES
Twisted Cord Band, p. 116

Make 1 (M1) increase, p. 108

Right and left-leaning decreases, p. 109

The "gap" on heel turn, p. 111

RIBBING
K1, p2, k1tbl, p2, k1tbl, p2, k1; repeat from * to * around.

LEG, WOMEN'S HEEL, MEN'S HEEL, INSTEP MEN'S
See Booklet, p. 5.

INSTRUCTIONS

TWISTED CORD BAND
CO 5 sts and work 18 rows in stockinette, always knitting the first and last st as edge sts. Cut yarn and leave the sts on the flexible cable on the circular. Make 12 (14) stips the same way. Slide the strips down to the end of the needle so that they can be worked in st st on the right side of the fabric.

Knot the first two strips:

Place the cast on stitches of the second strip onto an extra needle and rotate once clockwise. Then knit together one st of the first strip together with one cast on st of the second strip. The stitches on both needles should present stockinette stitch on the right side of the fabric.

Bring the stitches from the first strip around the second, from back to front. Then, knit each st of the second strip together with each cast on edge stitch of the first stitch. Again, be sure that when you knit the pieces together, both stockinette stitch sides present as the right sides.

Continue working in this way, knotting two strips as you go.

Divide the sts from all of the bands onto dpn or circulars and then work 5 rows back and forth in garter st over the 60 (70) sts.

RIBBING AND LEG
Work the first 30 (36) sts in ribbing. With the second circular, work the remaining 30 (34) sts in ribbing and then join to work in the round, being careful not to twist cast-on row. Work 12 rnds in ribbing pattern. Continue in leg pattern, working the 10-stitch repeat 6 times on each round (7 times per round).

Work a total of 48 rounds in pattern (4 x Rows 1-12).

(30+30/35+35 sts)

Men's sizes only: Before beginning the heel, with ndl 2 work 3 more sts from ndl 1, and slip the first 2 sts of ndl 2 to ndl 1 (30+30/34+36 sts).

HEEL
The heel is worked back and forth across the 30 (34) sts on ndl 1.

Row 1 (RS): M1, work 30 (34) sts in heel pattern, M1. (32/36 heel sts)

Row 2 (WS): K1, work 30 (34) sts in heel pattern (watch out for the twisted purl sts!), k1.

Row 3: K1, work 30 (34) sts in heel pattern, k1.

Continue working heel pattern until there are 28 (32) rows, ending with a WS row.

Turn heel:

Row 1 (RS): K17 (19), ssk, k1; turn.

Row 2 (WS): Sl 1 purlwise, p3, p2tog, p1; turn.

Row 3: Sl 1 pwise, knit until 1 st before the gap, ssk, k1; turn.

Row 4: Sl 1 pwise, purl until 1 st before the gap, p2tog, p1; turn.

Work Rows 3-4 another 5 (6) times until 18 (20) sts remain on heel.

GUSSET

Rnd 1:

Ndl 1: K18 (20) heel sts, pick up and knit 14 (16) sts along side of heel flap.

Ndl 2: Women's: work 3 repeats of leg pattern (Men's: work in Instep pattern).

Rnd 2:

Ndl 1: Pick up and knit 14 (16) sts along heel flap, k32 (36).

Ndl 2: Work in Leg (Instep) pattern following chart.

(46+30/52+36) sts

Rnd 3:

Ndl 1: K1, ssk, knit to last 3 sts on ndl and end with k2tog, k1.

Ndl 2: Work in Leg (Instep) pattern following chart.

Rnds 4 and 5:

Ndl 1: Knit.

Ndl 2: Work in Leg (Instep) pattern following chart.

Repeat Rnds 3-5 another 7 (8) times. (30+30/34+36) sts

FOOT

Ndl 1: Knit.

Ndl 2: Work in Leg (Instep) pattern following chart.

For sizes 36+37, work 5 pattern repeats after the heel; for sizes 38-45 work 6 pattern repeats. For all sizes, continue in stockinette over all sts until foot is desired length to toe (see Table).

BAND TOE

For Men's sizes, slip the last st on ndl 2 to ndl 1. (30+30/35+35 sts)

Shaping:

Ndl 1: K1, ssk, knit until 3 sts remain on needle and end with k2tog, k1.

Ndl 2: Work as for Ndl 1.

Continue around in stockinette, decreasing for Women's sizes as follows:

Knit 3 rnds and decrease on Rnd 4.

(Knit 2 rnds and dec on Rnd 3) 2 times.

Knit 1 rnd and dec on rnd 2) 3 times

Decrease on each of the next 6 rnds.

For Men's sizes, decrease as follows:

Knit 3 rnds and decrease on Rnd 4.

(Knit 2 rnds and dec on Rnd 3) 3 times.

Knit 1 rnd and dec on rnd 2) 4 times

Decrease on each of the next 6 rnds.

FINISHING

Cut yarn and thread end onto tapestry needle. Pull end through remaining 8 (10) sts. Pull tight and then weave in all ends neatly on WS.

Make the second sock the same way.

For Men's socks without the Twisted Cord Band, CO 70 sts, dividing sts 35-35 over two circulars and begin with Ribbing and Leg.

Shoe size: U.S. (Euro)	5-6 (36)	6-7 (37)	7-8 (38)	8-9 (39)	9-10 (40)	10-11 (41)	11-12 (42)	Men's 9 (43)	Men's 10 ½ (44)	Men's 11 ½ (45)
Foot length	9 ½ in	9 ½ in	9 ½-9 ¾ in	10 in	10 ¼ in	10 ½-10 ¾ in	10 ¾ in	11 in	11 ¼-11 ½ in	11 ½ in
	(23.5 cm)	(24 cm)	(24.5-25 cm)	(25.5 cm)	(26 cm)	(26.5-27 cm)	(27.5 cm)	(28 cm)	(28.5-29 cm)	(29.5 cm)
Sock length heel to toe	7 ¼ in	7 ½ in	7 ¾-8 in	8 in	8 ¼ in in	8 ½-8 ¾ in	8 ¾ in	8 ¾ in	9-9 ¼ in	9 ½ in
	(18.5 cm)	(19 cm)	(19.5-20 cm)	(20.5 cm)	(21 cm)	(21.5-22 cm)	(22.5 cm)	(22.5 cm)	(23-23.5 cm)	(24.5 cm)

Pink Strawflowers

It's getting warmer! You'll be pretty in pink wearing these strawflower pattern socks. Made with bamboo, you'll enjoy knitting them as well using this lovely yarn.

Pink Strawflowers

LEVEL OF DIFFICULTY
Intermediate

SIZES
Women's U.S. 5-6, 6-7, 7-8, 8-9, 9-10, 10-11, 11-12 (European 36, 37, 38, 39, 40, 41, 42)

Leg circumference: 8 ¼-11 in (21-28 cm)

Foot circumference: 8-9 ¾ in (20-25 cm)

The length of the sock can be determined by using the respective shoe size.

MATERIALS
Yarn: Fingering (CYCA #1), Trekking Pro Natura (75% wool/25% bamboo; 459 yd/100 g), Pink (#1544), 100 g

Needles: set of 5 dpn U.S. size 0 or 1.5 (2 or 2.5 mm) or size needed to obtain gauge

Extra needle for picking up sts to join picot edging

Stitch markers

Tapestry needle

GAUGE
32 sts and 42 rows in stockinette and lace pattern = 4 x 4 in (10 x 10 cm)

KNITTING BOOKLET
Charts, p. 5

TECHNIQUES
Right- and left-leaning decreases, p. 109

The "gap" on heel turn, p. 111

LACE PATTERN FOR LEG
See Booklet, p. 5.

On even-numbered rounds (not charted), knit all sts around, including yarnovers. On Rnd 4, slip the last st of each dpn to the next ndl. Knit the last st on ndls 1, 2, and 3; the last st on ndl 4 is decreased with the first st of ndl 1 on Rnd 5.

INSTEP
See Booklet, p. 5.

INSTRUCTIONS

PICOT EDGING

CO 64 sts. Divide sts onto 4 dpn with 16 sts on each ndl. Join, being careful not to twist cast-on row.

Knit 6 rnds.

Next rnd: *K2tog, yo; repeat from * around.

Knit 7 rounds.

Ndl 1: Using an extra dpn and working on WS, pick up 16 loops from cast-on row, making sure that picked up sts are directly below live sts. Place ndl with picked up loops behind needle with live sts and then join the sets of sts together with k2tog around.

Ndls 2, 3, 4: Work as for Ndl 1.

Knit 1 round.

(16+16+16+16 sts)

LEG

Ndl 1: Work 16 sts in lace pattern for leg (see chart) (= 2 pattern repeats).

Ndls 2, 3, 4: Work as for ndl 1.

Work a total of 48 rounds in leg pattern (4 x Rnds 1-12).

(16+16+16+16 sts)

To set up the heel pattern, slip the 1st st of ndl 3 to ndl 2.

(16+17+15+16 sts)

HEEL

Move the sts on ndls 3 and 4 onto one needle. Work the heel over these 31 sts. Work back and forth in stockinette for 31 rows, beginning on WS.

Set sts on ndls 1 and 2 aside for instep while you work the heel.

(31 heel sts)

Turn heel:

Row 1 (RS): K16, ssk, k1; turn.

Row 2 (WS): Sl 1 purlwise, p2, p2tog, p1; turn.

Row 3: Sl 1 pwise, knit until 1 st before the gap, ssk, k1; turn.

Row 4: Sl 1 pwise, purl until 1 st before the gap, p2tog, p1; turn.

Work Rows 3-4 another 5 times until you've worked the same number of decreases on both sides of the ndl and 17 sts remain on heel.

FOOT

Rnd 1:

Ndl 4: Sl 1 pwise, k16, pick up and knit 15 sts along side of heel flap.

Ndls 1 and 2: Work across on Row 1 of instep pattern.

Ndl 3: Pick up and knit 15 sts along side of heel flap and then k8 from ndl 1.

Ndl 4: K24.

(16+17+23+24 sts)

Rnd 2:

Ndls 1 and 2: Work in instep pattern.

Ndls 3 and 4: Knit.

Rnd 3:

Ndls 1 and 2: Work in instep pattern.

Ndl 3: K1, ssk, knit rem sts.

Ndl 4: Knit until 3 sts remain on ndl and end with k2tog, k1.

Rnds 4 and 5:

Ndls 1 and 2: Work in instep pattern.

Ndls 3 and 4: Knit.

Repeat Rnds 3-5 another 7 times.

(16+17+15+16 sts)

Continue in stockinette on sole and lace pattern on instep until foot is 2 in (5 cm) less than total foot length (see Table).

To end the pattern most attractively, finish with Row 2 or Row 8.

BAND TOE

Set-up for toe shaping:

Knit 2 rounds over all sts. Slip the last st on ndl 2 back to ndl 3.

(16+16+16+16 sts)

Shaping:

Ndl 1: K1, ssk, knit rem sts on ndl.

Ndl 2: Knit until 3 sts remain on ndl and end with k2tog, k1.

Ndl 3: Work as for ndl 1.

Ndl 4: Work as for ndl 2.

Knit 3 rnds and decrease on Rnd 4.

(Knit 2 rnds and dec on Rnd 3) 2 times.

Knit 1 rnd and dec on rnd 2) 4 times

Decrease on each of the next 6 rnds.

FINISHING

Cut yarn and thread end onto tapestry needle. Pull end through remaining 8 sts. Pull tight and then weave in all ends neatly on WS.

Make the second sock the same way.

Shoe size: U.S. (Euro)	5-6 (36)	6-7 (37)	7-8 (38)	8-9 (39)	9-10 (40)	10-11 (41)	11-12 (42)
Foot length	9 ½ in	9 ½ in	9 ½-9 ¾ in	10 in	10 ¼ in	10 ½-10 ¾ in	10 ¾ in
	(23.5 cm)	(24 cm)	(24.5-25 cm)	(25.5 cm)	(26 cm)	(26.5-27 cm)	(27.5 cm)
Sock length heel to toe	7 ¼ in	7 ½ in	7 ¾-8 in	8 in	8 ¼ in	8 ½-8 ¾ in	8 ¾ in
	(18.5 cm)	(19 cm)	(19.5-20 cm)	(20.5 cm)	(21 cm)	(21.5-22 cm)	(22.5 cm)

Colors of Provence

Spring is in the air and brings with it the sweet smell of lavender. Imagine walking through rows of purple blooms, one of the colors in this designer yarn. Kaffe Fasset has created a yarn with three colors perfectly representing the colors of lavender, the earth and the sky.

Lavender

Colors of Provence

LEVEL OF DIFFICULTY
Intermediate

SIZES
Women's U.S. 5-6, 6-7, 7-8, 8-9, 9-10, 10-11, 11-12 (European 36, 37, 38, 39, 40, 41, 42)

Leg circumference: 8-10 ¼ in (20-26 cm)

Foot circumference: 8 ¾ -11 ½ in (22-29 cm)

The length of the sock can be determined by using the respective shoe size.

MATERIALS
Yarn: Fingering (CYCA #1), Regia Design Line (75% wool/25% nylon; 229 yd/50 g), Landscape amazonas (#4354), 100 g

Needles: 2 circulars U.S. size 0 or 1.5 (2 or 2.5 mm) or size needed to obtain gauge

Cable needle

Tapestry needle

GAUGE
32 sts and 42 rows in stockinette = 4 x 4 in (10 x 10 cm)

34 sts and 42 rows in cable pattern = 4 x 4 in (10 x 10 cm)

KNITTING BOOKLET
Chart, p. 4

TECHNIQUES
Make 1 (M1) increase, p. 108

Right- and left-leaning decreases, p. 109

The "gap" on heel turn, p. 111

RIBBING
K1tbl, p1; rep from around.

CABLE PATTERN
See Booklet, p. 4.

INSTRUCTIONS

CO 70 sts and divide them over the 2 circulars, with 35 sts on each ndl. Join, being careful not to twist cast-on row.

Ndl 1: Work 26 sts in Ribbing, 9 sts in cable pattern.
Ndl 2: Work as for ndl 1.

Work 18 rnds as set = 2 x Rnds 1-9 of cable pattern.
(35+35 sts)

LEG
Ndl 1: K25, p1, work 9 sts in cable pattern.
Ndl 2: Work as for Ndl 1.

Work 36 rnds as set = 4 x Rnds 1-9 of cable pattern.

Ndl 1: K25, p1, work 9 sts of Rnd 1 of cable pattern.
Ndl 2: Work 35 sts in cable pattern, M1, and work last st in cable pattern.
(35+36 sts)

Ndl 1: K25, p1, work 9 sts of Rnd 2 of cable pattern.
Ndl 2: Work 36 sts of Rnd 2 of cable pattern.

Ndl 1: K25, p1, 9 sts in cable pattern.
Ndl 2: Work 36 sts in cable pattern.

Work a total of 18 rnds as set (2 x Rnds 1-9 of cable pattern).
(35+36 sts)

HEEL

Rnd 1:

Ndl 1: K25, p1, M1, work 9 sts in cable pattern.

Ndl 2: Work 36 sts in cable pattern, increasing with M1 before the last purl st and then end with p1.

Rnd 2:

Ndl 1: K25, purl to cable pattern and then end with 9 sts in cable pattern.

Ndl 2: Work 36 sts in cable pattern and purl rem sts on ndl.

Rnd 3:

Ndl 1: K25, p1, M1, purl to cable pattern, work 9 sts in cable pattern.

Ndl 2: Work 36 sts in cable pattern, purl to last st and end with M1, p1.

Repeat Rnds 2 and 3 another 13 times
(50+51 sts)

Ndl 1: K25; the remaining sts will be knit onto ndl 2.

Turn heel with short rows on ndl 2:

Row 1 (RS): Knit rem 25 sts on ndl 1, k14 sts on ndl 2, ssk, k1; turn.

Row 2 (WS): Sl 1 purlwise, p3, p2tog, p1; turn.

Row 3: Sl 1 pwise, knit until 1 st before the gap, ssk, k1; turn.

Row 4: Sl 1 pwise, purl until 1 st before the gap, p2tog, p1; turn.

Repeat Rows 3 and 4 another 16 times until the same number of decreases have been worked on both sides of the needle and 40 sts remain.
(25+40)

On the next RS row with ndl 2, k25, and knit the remaining 4 sts on ndl 2 with ndl 1.

Continue working in rounds.

Rnd 1:

Ndl 1: Knit the last 4 sts on ndl 2, k25, knit 4 sts from ndl 2.

Ndl 2: K32.
(33+32 sts)

Rnd 2:

Ndl 1: K2, ssk, k25, k2tog, k2.

Ndl 2: K32.
(31+32 sts)

FOOT

Work in stockinette over all the sts around until foot is 2 in (5 cm) less than total foot length (see Table).

BAND TOE

Shaping:

Ndl 1: K1, ssk, knit to last 3 sts on ndl and end k2tog, k1.

Ndl 2: Work as for ndl 1.

Knit 3 rnds and decrease on Rnd 4.
(Knit 2 rnds and dec on Rnd 3) 2 times.
Knit 1 rnd and dec on rnd 2) 4 times
Decrease on each of the next 5 rnds.

Last decrease rnd:

Ndl 1: K2, k2tog, k1.

Ndl 2: K1, ssk, knit to last 3 sts and end with k2tog, k1.

FINISHING

Cut yarn and thread end onto tapestry needle. Pull end through remaining 8 sts. Pull tight and then weave in all ends neatly on WS.

Make the second sock the same way.

Shoe size: U.S. (Euro)	5-6 (36)	6-7 (37)	7-8 (38)	8-9 (39)	9-10 (40)	10-11 (41)	11-12 (42)
Foot length	9 ½ in	9 ½ in	9 ½-9 ¾ in	10 in	10 ¼ in	10 ½-10 ¾ in	10 ¾ in
	(23.5 cm)	(24 cm)	(24.5-25 cm)	(25.5 cm)	(26 cm)	(26.5-27 cm)	(27.5 cm)
Sock length heel to toe	7 ¼ in	7 ½ in	7 ¾-8 in	8 in	8 ¼ in in	8 ½-8 ¾ in	8 ¾ in
	(18.5 cm)	(19 cm)	(19.5-20 cm)	(20.5 cm)	(21 cm)	(21.5-22 cm)	(22.5 cm)

Summer Fresh

Dance into the summer night as gracefully
as the starfish swirling around these cool
blue socks.

Summer Fresh

LEVEL OF DIFFICULTY
Intermediate

SIZES
Women's U.S. 5-6, 6-7, 7-8, 8-9, 9-10, 10-11, 11-12 (European 36, 37, 38, 39, 40, 41, 42)

Leg circumference: 8 ¼-10 ¾ in (21-27 cm)

Foot circumference: 8-9 ¾ in (20-25 cm)

The length of the sock can be determined by using the respective shoe size.

MATERIALS
Yarn: Fingering (CYCA #1), Trekking Uni (75% wool/25% nylon; 462 yd/100 g), Light blue (#1467), 100 g

Needles: 2 circulars U.S. size 0 or 1.5 (2 or 2.5 mm) or size needed to obtain gauge

Crochet hook: U.S. B-C (2.5 mm)

2 additional dpns to be used as cable needles

Tapestry needle

GAUGE
32 sts and 40 rows in stockinette = 4 x 4 in (10 x 10 cm)

35 sts and 40 rows in leg pattern = 4 x 4 in (10 x 10 cm)

KNITTING BOOKLET
Charts, p. 6

TECHNIQUES
Right- and left-leaning decreases, p. 109

The "gap" on heel turn, p. 111

RIBBING
K1tbl, p1; rep from around.

LEG PATTERN
See booklet, p. 6. On all the even-numbered rounds, knit the knit sts and the yarnovers and purl the purl sts.

To work the cable at needle changes on Rnd 13, work cable crossing with the last 4 sts of the needle and the first 2 sts of the next ndl. To keep the stitch counts even, work the last 2 sts of the cable with the next needle. (Work the cable crossing the same way on on Rnd 27.)

INSTEP PATTERN
See booklet, p. 6.

INSTRUCTIONS

CO 70 sts and arrange with 35 sts on each circular; join, being careful not to twist cast-on row. Work 14 rnds in k1tbl, p1 rib.

Now work the leg pattern with a total of 5 pattern repeats. Arrange sts with 2 ½ pattern repeats on each needle; needle 2 begins with the 2nd half of a repeat.
Work a total of 56 rnds in pattern (2 x Rnds 1-28). On Rnd 56, do not work the last st of needle 2.

Arrange sts for the heel: slip the last st of needle 1 onto needle 2 and slip the last st of needle 2 onto needle 1 (35+35 sts).

HEEL
Work the heel with ndl 1:
Row 1 (RS): K35; turn.
Row 2 (WS): K3, p29, k2; turn.
Repeat Rows 1-2 another 14 times.

Turn Heel:
Row 1 (RS): K20, ssk, k1; turn.
Row 2 (WS): Sl 1 pwise, p6, p2 tog, p1; turn.
Row 3: Sl 1 pwise, knit until 1 st before the gap, ssk, k1; turn.
Row 4: Sl 1 pwise, purl until 1 st before the gap, p2tog, p1; turn.
Repeat Rows 3 and 4 5 more times, until decreases are complete on both sides of the needle and 21 heel sts remain.

FOOT

Rnd 1:

Ndl 1: Sl 1, k20, pick up and knit 15 sts along side of heel flap.

Ndl 2: Work across instep sts in pattern. (36+35 sts).

Rnd 2:

Ndl 1: Pick up and knit 15 sts along side of heel flap, k36.

Ndl 2: Work in pattern across instep sts. (51+35 sts).

Rnds 3-4:

Ndl 1: Knit in stockinette.

Ndl 2: Work in pattern across instep sts.

Rnd 5:

Ndl 1: K1, ssk, knit until 3 sts remain and end with k2tog, k1.

Ndl 2: Work in pattern across instep sts.

Repeat Rnds 3-5 another 9 times. (31+35 sts).

Rnd 33:

Ndl 1: K31.

Ndl 2: Work in pattern across instep sts.

Continue in pattern, working the number of repeats for your size:

For shoe sizes U.S. 6-9 (36-39), work another 38 rnds (1 x Rnds 5-28 and 1 x Rnds 1-14);

For shoe sizes U.S. 9-12 (40-42), work another 52 rnds (1 x Rnds 5-28 and 1 x Rnds 1-28).

Shaping

Ndl 1: K31.

Ndl 2:

For sizes U.S. 6-9 (36-39), K12, ssk, k2tog, k10, ssk, k2tog, k5.

For sizes U.S. 9-12 (40-42): K5, ssk, k2tog, k10, ssk, k2tog, k12.

(31+31 sts).

Continue in stockinette over all the sts until foot is 2 in (5 cm) less than total foot length (see table).

BAND TOE

Shaping:

Ndl 1: K1, ssk, knit until 3 sts remain on ndl and end with k2tog, k1.

Ndl 2: Work as for ndl 1.

Continue in stockinette, decreasing as follows:

Knit 3 rnds and decrease on Rnd 4.

(Knit 2 rnds and dec on Rnd 3) 2 times.

Knit 1 rnd and dec on rnd 2) 2 times

Decrease on each of the next 5 rnds.

FINISHING

Finish by joining rem 10 sts with Kitchener st.

Cut yarn and weave in all ends neatly on WS.

Make the second sock the same way.

Shoe size: U.S. (Euro)	5-6 (36)	6-7 (37)	7-8 (38)	8-9 (39)	9-10 (40)	10-11 (41)	11-12 (42)
Foot length	9 ½ in	9 ½ in	9 ½-9 ¾ in	10 in	10 ¼ in	10 ½-10 ¾ in	10 ¾ in
	(23.5 cm)	(24 cm)	(24.5-25 cm)	(25.5 cm)	(26 cm)	(26.5-27 cm)	(27.5 cm)
Sock length heel to toe	7 ¼ in	7 ½ in	7 ¾-8 in	8 in	8 ¼ in in	8 ½-8 ¾ in	8 ¾ in
	(18.5 cm)	(19 cm)	(19.5-20 cm)	(20.5 cm)	(21 cm)	(21.5-22 cm)	(22.5 cm)

Rambling Green

As green as green can be. The roses stretch up to the sun. This leaf pattern with its perky bobbles is open enough for your feet to catch a quick glimpse of sunshine on a hot summer day.

Rambling Green

LEVEL OF DIFFICULTY
Intermediate

SIZES
Women's U.S. 5-6, 6-7, 7-8, 8-9, 9-10, 10-11, 11-12 (European 36, 37, 38, 39, 40, 41, 42)

Leg circumference: 8 ¼-10 ¼ in (21-26 cm)

Foot circumference: 8-9 ½ in (20-24 cm)

The length of the sock can be determined by using the respective shoe size.

MATERIALS
Yarn: Fingering (CYCA #1), Trekking Pro Natura (75% wool/25% bambo; 459 yd/100 g), Green (#1506), 100 g

Needles: set of 5 dpn U.S. size 0 or 1.5 (2 or 2.5 mm) or size needed to obtain gauge

Tapestry needle

GAUGE
32 sts and 42 rows in stockinette = 4 x 4 in (10 x 10 cm)

33 sts and 42 rows in leaf pattern = 4 x 4 in (10 x 10 cm)

KNITTING BOOKLET
Chart, p. 6

TECHNIQUES
Right- and left-leaning decreases, p. 109

Crocheted bobbles, p. 115

The "gap" on heel turn, p. 111

Bead knitting, p. 117

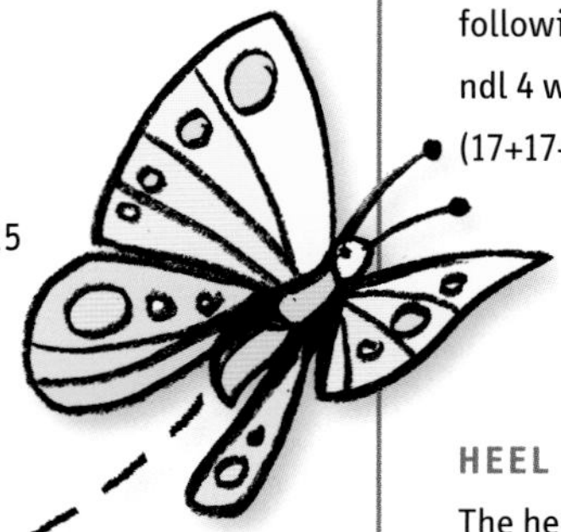

LEAF PATTERN
See Booklet, p. 6.

RIBBING
Work following Row 0 on chart.

INSTRUCTIONS

CO 68 sts and divide evenly onto 4 dpn with 17 sts on each ndl; join, being careful not to twist cast-on row. Work 16 rnds in ribbing following row 0 on chart.

LEG
Ndl 1: Work 17 sts in leg pattern following chart (1 repeat), beginning on Rnd 1 for the right sock and beginning on Rnd 11 for the left sock.
Ndls 2, 3, 4: Work as for Ndl 1.

Work 49 rnds in leg pattern (right sock: 2 x Rnds 1-20 and 1 x Rnds 1-9; left sock: 1 x Rnds 11-20 and 1 x Rnds 1-20, and then 1 x Rnds 1-19). With Ndls 1, 2, 3, work Rnd 10 (left sock, work Rnd 20) following the chart. On the last rnd, the sts of ndl 4 will be worked as part of the heel (17+17+17+17 sts).

HEEL
The heel is worked back and forth across the sts of ndls 1 and 4. Set aside sts on ndls 2 and 3 — they will be used later for the instep.

Row 1 (RS): K1, *p1, k1tbl; rep from * another 6 times, p1, k2tog; *p1, k1tbl; rep from * another 6 times, p1, k1. (33 heel sts)
Row 2 (WS): K1, *k1, p1tbl, rep from * another 14 times, k2.
Row 3: K1, *p1, k1tbl, rep from * another 14 times, p1, k1.
Row 4: K1, *k1, p1 tbl, rep from * another 14 times, k2.
Repeat Rows 3-4 another 13 times. There should be a total of 30 rows and 33 heel sts.

Turn Heel:
Row 1 (RS): K18, ssk, k1; turn.
Row 2(WS): Sl 1 pwise, p6, p2 tog, p1; turn.
Row 3: Sl 1 pwise, knit until 1 st before the gap, ssk, k1; turn.
Row 4: Sl 1 pwise, purl until 1 st before the gap, p2tog, p1; turn.
Repeat rows 3 and 4 another 5 times, until decreases are complete on both sides of the needle and 19 heel sts remain.

FOOT
Rnd 1:
Ndl 1: Sl 1, k18, pick up and knit 15 sts along side of heel flap.
Ndls 2 and 3: Work across the 17 sts of each ndl in pattern following chart, beginning with Row 1 for the right sock and Row 11 for the left sock.
Ndl 4: Pick up and knit 15 sts along heel flap, k9. (25+17+17+24 sts)

Rnd 2:

Ndl 1: Knit.

Ndls 2 and 3: Continue in leaf pattern.

Ndl 4: Knit.

Rnd 3:

Ndl 1: Knit until 3 sts remain and end k2tog, k1.

Ndls 2 and 3: Continue in leaf pattern.

Ndl 4: K1, ssk, knit to end of ndl.

Rnds 4-5:

Ndl 1: Knit.

Ndls 2 and 3: Continue in leaf pattern.

Ndl 4: Knit.

Repeat Rnds 3-5 another 7 times.
(17+17+17+16 sts)

Continue in stockinette on sole and pattern on instep until desired foot length minus 2 in (5 cm) is reached (see table).
To end the pattern most attractively, finish with Row 10 or Row 20.

BAND TOE

Rnd 1 (transition to toe pattern):

Ndl 1: *K1tbl, p1; rep from * another 6 times, k1tbl, k2.

Ndl 2: K2, *K1tbl, p1; rep from * another 6 times, and end by knitting the last st on ndl 2 with the first st on ndl 3.

Ndl 3: *P1, k1tbl; rep from * another 6 times, k2.

Ndl 4: K2, *k1 tbl, p1; rep from * another 6 times.
(17+17+16+16 sts)

Rnd 2:

Ndl 1: *K1tbl, p1; rep from * another 6 times, k1tbl, k2.

Ndl 2: K2, *K1tbl, p1; rep from * another 6 times, end with k1tbl.

Ndl 3: *P1, k1tbl; rep from * another 6 times, k2.

Ndl 4: K2, *k1 tbl, p1; rep from * another 6 times.
(17+17+16+16 sts)

Rnd 3 Decreases:

Ndl 1: Work in rib pattern as set until 3 sts rem on ndl and end with k2tog, k1.

Ndl 2: K1, ssk, work rem sts in rib pattern.

Ndl 3: Work as for Ndl 1.

Ndl 4: Work as for Ndl 2.

Continue in pattern, decreasing as follows:
Knit 3 rnds and decrease on Rnd 4.
(Knit 2 rnds and dec on Rnd 3) 3 times.
Knit 1 rnd and dec on rnd 2) 3 times
Decrease on each of the next 6 rnds.
On every other rnd, the outermost edge sts (the last 2 sts on ndls 1 and 3 and the first 2 sts on ndls 2 and 4) are knit; the remaining sts are worked in k1tbl, p1 rib.

FINISHING

Cut yarn and thread end onto tapestry needle.
Pull end through rem 10 sts and pull tight.
Weave in all ends neatly on WS.

Make the second sock the same way.

If you are going to wear the socks in close-fitting shoes, you can substitute the bobbles for purl stitches on the instep. If desired, you can knit in small seed beads to replace the bobbles.

Shoe size: U.S. (Euro)	5-6 (36)	6-7 (37)	7-8 (38)	8-9 (39)	9-10 (40)	10-11 (41)	11-12 (42)
Foot length	9 ½ in	9 ½ in	9 ½-9 ¾ in	10 in	10 ¼ in	10 ½-10 ¾ in	10 ¾ in
	(23.5 cm)	(24 cm)	(24.5-25 cm)	(25.5 cm)	(26 cm)	(26.5-27 cm)	(27.5 cm)
Sock length heel to toe	7 ¼ in	7 ½ in	7 ¾-8 in	8 in	8 ¼ in in	8 ½-8 ¾ in	8 ¾ in
	(18.5 cm)	(19 cm)	(19.5-20 cm)	(20.5 cm)	(21 cm)	(21.5-22 cm)	(22.5 cm)

Flower Pattern

A little light stitch-play for a hot day! Daisies are often the first signs of summer. The flower buds have already made their big debut. Wear these sunny yellow socks to brighten up your day!

Flower Pattern

LEVEL OF DIFFICULTY
Intermediate

SIZES
Women's U.S. 5-6, 6-7, 7-8, 8-9, 9-10, 10-11, 11-12 (European 36, 37, 38, 39, 40, 41, 42)

Leg circumference: 8 ¼-10 ¼ in (21-26 cm)

Foot circumference: 8-9 ½ in (20-24 cm)

The length of the sock can be determined by using the respective shoe size.

MATERIALS
Yarn: Fingering (CYCA #1), Trekking Pro Natura (75% wool/25% bamboo; 459 yd/100 g), Yellow (#1547), 100 g

Needles: set of 5 dpn U.S. size 0 or 1.5 (2 or 2.5 mm) or size needed to obtain gauge

Tapestry needle

GAUGE
32 sts and 42 rows in stockinette and lace patterns = 4 x 4 in (10 x 10 cm)

KNITTING BOOKLET
Charts, p. 7

TECHNIQUES
Right- and left-leaning decreases, p. 109

Make 1 (M1), p. 108

The "gap" on heel turn, p. 111

RIBBING
K1tbl, p1; rep from around.

LEG, INSTEP, AND FOOT PATTERN
See Booklet, p. 7.

INSTRUCTIONS

CO 64 sts and divide onto 4 dpn with 16 sts on each ndl; join, being careful not to twist cast-on row. Work 16 rnds in k1tbl, p1 rib. (16+16+16+16 sts)

LEG
Ndl 1: Work 16 sts in leg pattern (2 repeats).
Ndls 2, 3, 4: Work as for Ndl 1.
Work 28 rnds in leg pattern (1 x Rnds 1-16 and then 1 x Rnds 1-12).
If you want to lengthen or shorten the leg, you must always omit or add a complete repeat of 16 rnds.

HEEL
Continue working around when working the heel.
Ndls 1, 2, 3: Work 16 sts each in leg pattern.
Ndl 4: Work heel following heel chart in Booklet.
Work a total of 32 rnds as set (16+16+16+42)
To make the instep symmetrical on both sides, slip the last st on ndl 1 to ndl 2.
(15+17+16+42)

Work the heel back and forth over the 57 sts on ndls 4 and 1. On the 2nd row, move the sts of ndls 1 and 4 onto one needle.

Row 1 (half RS row): Knit 15 sts on ndl 1; turn.
Row 2 (WS): Sl 1pwise, p29, p2tog, p1; turn.
Row 3: Sl 1pwise, k4, ssk, k1; turn.
Row 4: Sl 1, purl until 1 st before the gap, p2tog, p1; turn.
Row 5: Sl 1, knit until 1 st before the gap, ssk, k1; turn.
Repeat Rows 4-5 another 11 times and then work Row 4 once more until the decreases on both sides are complete and 31 sts remain.
For sizes U.S. 5-7 (Euro 36-38) work 2 rows in stockinette, with k2tog at the end of each row. (29 heel sts remain)

FOOT
Rnd 1:
Ndl 1: Knit.
Ndls 2 and 3: Work 33 sts on instep pattern.
Ndl 4: Knit.
(Sizes U.S. 5-7 / Euro 36-38: 14+17+16+15 sts).
(Sizes U.S. 8-12 / Euro 39-42: 15+17+16+16 sts).

Continue in pattern as set until foot is 2 in (5 cm) less than total foot length (see Table). If possible, end the lace pattern on the foot on either Row 8 or 16.

BAND TOE

Work 2 rnds in stockinette and slip the first st on ndl 2 to ndl 1.

(Sizes U.S. 5-7 / Euro 36-38: 15+16+16+15 sts).

(Sizes U.S. 8-12 / Euro 39-42: 16+16+16+16 sts).

Note: For sizes U.S. 5-7 / Euro 36-38 on the first row only, omit the decreases on ndls 1 and 4 and simply knit across. Decrease on all following rows as described below.

Toe Shaping

Ndl 1: Knit until 3 sts remain and end with k2tog, k1.

Ndl 2: K1, ssk, knit remaining sts.

Ndl 3: Knit until 3 sts remain and end with k2tog, k1.

Ndl 4: K1, ssk, knit remaining sts.

Knit 3 rnds and decrease on Rnd 4.

(Knit 2 rnds and dec on Rnd 3) 2 times.

Knit 1 rnd and dec on rnd 2) 4 times

Decrease on each of the next 6 rnds.

FINISHING

Cut yarn, thread end onto tapestry needle and pull yarn through rem 8 sts. Pull tight and then weave in all ends neatly on WS.

Make the other sock the same way.

Shoe size: U.S. (Euro)	5-6 (36)	6-7 (37)	7-8 (38)	8-9 (39)	9-10 (40)	10-11 (41)	11-12 (42)
Foot length	9 ½ in	9 ½ in	9 ½-9 ¾ in	10 in	10 ¼ in	10 ½-10 ¾ in	10 ¾ in
	(23.5 cm)	(24 cm)	(24.5-25 cm)	(25.5 cm)	(26 cm)	(26.5-27 cm)	(27.5 cm)
Sock length heel to toe	7 ¼ in	7 ½ in	7 ¾-8 in	8 in	8 ¼ in	8 ½-8 ¾ in	8 ¾ in
	(18.5 cm)	(19 cm)	(19.5-20 cm)	(20.5 cm)	(21 cm)	(21.5-22 cm)	(22.5 cm)

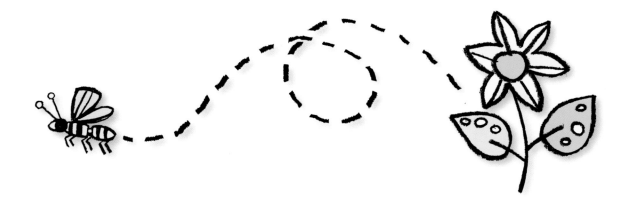

Dancing Leaves

A zephyr in heathery white: The pattern,

knit with a soft silk yarn, stretches upwards

into its canopy, a delightful summery frill.

Dancing Leaves

LEVEL OF DIFFICULTY
Intermediate

SIZES
Women's U.S. 5-6, 6-7, 7-8, 8-9, 9-10, 10-11, 11-12 (European 36, 37, 38, 39, 40, 41, 42)

Leg circumference: 8 ¼-10 ¾ in (21-27 cm)

Foot circumference: 8-9 ¾ in (20-25 cm)

The length of the sock can be determined by using the respective shoe size.

MATERIALS
Yarn: Fingering (CYCA #1), Regia Silk 4-ply (55% wool/25% nylon/20% silk; 219 yd/50 g), Linen heather (#05), 100 g

Needles: Set of 5 dpn U.S. size 0 or 2.5 (2 or 3 mm) or size needed to obtain gauge

Crochet hook: U.S. B-C (2.5 mm)

Tapestry needle

GAUGE
30 sts and 42 rows in stockinette = 4 x 4 in (10 x 10 cm)

KNITTING BOOKLET
Charts, p. 8

TECHNIQUES
Right- and left-leaning decreases, p. 109

Crocheted bobble, p. 115

The "gap" on heel turn, p. 111

LEG, INSTEP, AND HEEL PATTERN
See Booklet, p. 8.

INSTRUCTIONS

CO 134 sts divided on 4 ndls as follows: 30 sts on ndls 1, 2, and 3 and 44 sts on ndl 4. Join, being careful not to twist cast-on row.
Knit 8 rnds.
Rnd 9: K2tog around.
(15+15+15+22 sts)

Ndls 1, 2, and 3: Work Rnd 0 of leg pattern, followed by Rnds 1-12
Ndl 4: Work Rnds 1-12 of the leg pattern

LEG
Ndls 1, 2, 3: Work in leg pattern.
Ndl 4: Work in leg pattern for ndl 4.
Work in this pattern for 48 rnds.
(3 x Rnds 1-16)
(15+15+15+22 sts)

HEEL

In order to place the lace pattern symmetrically on both sides of the instep, slip the last 2 sts of ndl 1 onto ndl 2. The heel will be worked across sts on ndls 1 and 4.
(35 heel sts)

Row 1 (half row, RS):
Ndl 1: *K1tbl, p1; rep from *5 more times, k1tbl; turn.

Row 2 (WS):
Complete Row 2 of the heel pattern, then place sts of ndl 1 and 4 onto one ndl.
Continue back and forth in heel pattern for 30 rows total (3 x Rows 1-8 and 1 x Rows 1-6).

Turn Heel:
Row 1 (RS): K18, ssk, k1; turn.
Row 2 (WS): Sl 1 pwise, p2, p 2 tog, p1; turn.
Row 3: Sl 1 pwise, knit until 1 st before the gap, ssk, k1; turn.
Row 4: Sl 1 pwise, purl until 1 st before the gap, p2tog, p1; turn.
Repeat rows 3 and 4 6 more times, until decreases are complete on both sides of the needle and 19 heel sts remain.

FOOT
Rnd 1:
Ndl 1: Sl 1, k18, pick up and knit 15 sts along side of heel flap.
Ndl 2: P2, work 15 sts in leg and instep pattern.

Ndl 3: Work 15 sts in leg and instep pattern.
Ndl 4: Pick up and knit 15 sts along other side of heel flap, k9.
(25+17+15+ 24 sts)

Rnd 2:
Ndl 1: Knit.
Ndl 2: P2, work 15 sts in leg and instep pattern.
Ndl 3: Work 15 sts in leg and instep pattern.
Ndl 4: Knit.

Rnd 3:
Ndl 1: Knit until 3 sts rem on ndl and end k2tog, k1.
Ndl 2: P2, work 15 sts in leg and instep pattern.
Ndl 3: Work 15 sts in leg and instep pattern.
Ndl 4: K1, ssk, knit rem sts on ndl.

Rnds 4 and 5:
Ndl 1: Knit.
Ndl 2: P2, work 15 sts in leg and instep pattern.
Ndl 3: Work 15 sts in leg and instep pattern.
Ndl 4: Knit.

Repeat the last 3 rnds 7 more times.
(17+16+16+16 sts)

Ndl 1: Knit
Ndl 2: P2, work 15 sts in leg and instep pattern.
Ndl 3: Work 15 sts in leg and instep pattern.
Ndl 4: Knit.

Continue working in this way until foot is 2 in (5 cm) less than total foot length (see Table). In order to end the motif attractively, if possible end with Rnd 8 or 16.

BAND TOE

Knit 2 rnds, working k2tog at the beginning of ndl 1 on the first rnd.
(16+16+16+16 sts)

Toe Shaping
Ndl 1: Knit until 3 sts remain and end with k2tog, k1.
Ndl 2: K1, ssk, knit remaining sts.
Ndl 3: Work as for ndl 1.
Ndl 4: Work as for ndl 2.

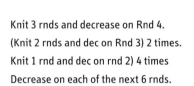

Knit 3 rnds and decrease on Rnd 4.
(Knit 2 rnds and dec on Rnd 3) 2 times.
Knit 1 rnd and dec on rnd 2) 4 times
Decrease on each of the next 6 rnds.

FINISHING

Cut yarn, thread end onto tapestry needle and pull yarn through rem 8 sts. Pull tight and then weave in all ends neatly on WS.

Make the other sock the same way.

Shoe size: U.S. (Euro)	5-6 (36)	6-7 (37)	7-8 (38)	8-9 (39)	9-10 (40)	10-11 (41)	11-12 (42)
Foot length	9 ½ in	9 ½ in	9 ½-9 ¾ in	10 in	10 ¼ in	10 ½-10 ¾ in	10 ¾ in
	(23.5 cm)	(24 cm)	(24.5-25 cm)	(25.5 cm)	(26 cm)	(26.5-27 cm)	(27.5 cm)
Sock length heel to toe	7 ¼ in	7 ½ in	7 ¾-8 in	8 in	8 ¼ in in	8 ½-8 ¾ in	8 ¾ in
	(18.5 cm)	(19 cm)	(19.5-20 cm)	(20.5 cm)	(21 cm)	(21.5-22 cm)	(22.5 cm)

Rhombus

Feel the warmth of summer. Nature's beautiful colors peak as the sun sets and shoots out fiery orange rays like a dragon breathing fire—a fantastic interplay of form and color.

Rhombus

LEVEL OF DIFFICULTY
Intermediate

SIZES
Women's U.S. 5-6, 6-7, 7-8, 8-9, 9-10, 10-11, 11-12 (European 36, 37, 38, 39, 40, 41, 42)

Leg circumference: 8 ¾-11 in (22-28 cm)

Foot circumference: 8 ¼-9 ¾ in (21-25 cm)

The length of the sock can be determined by using the respective shoe size.

MATERIALS
Yarn: Fingering (CYCA #1), Trekking Pro Natura (75% wool/25% bamboo; 459 yd/100 g), Red (#1546), 100 g

Needles: set of 5 dpn U.S. size 0 or 1.5 (2 or 2.5 mm) or size needed to obtain gauge

Tapestry needle

GAUGE
32 sts and 40 rows in stockinette and lace patterns = 4 x 4 in (10 x 10 cm)

KNITTING BOOKLET
Charts, p. 8

TECHNIQUES
Right- and left-leaning decreases, p. 109

The "gap" on heel turn, p. 111

LEG AND INSTEP PATTERN
See booklet, p. 8.

INSTRUCTIONS

CO 64 sts and divide onto 4 dpn with 16 sts on each ndl; join, being careful not to twist cast-on row. Work 15 rnds in k2, p2 rib.

LEG
Note Only the odd-numbered pattern rows are shown on the chart. Knit all even-numbered rows.

Work 72 rounds (= 2 repeats of the 36-row pattern) in rhombus pattern following chart.

Now slip the first st on ndl 4 to ndl 3 so that the instep pattern will be symmetrical. (16+16+17+15 sts)

HEEL
Work the heel back and forth over sts on ndls 1 and 4, moving all the heel sts to one needle. Set sts on ndls 2 and 3 (instep sts) aside while you work the heel.

Row 1 (half row, RS): Ndl 1: k16; turn.
Row 2 (WS row): Ndls 1 and 4: K3, p25, k3; turn.
Row 3: Knit across.
Row 4: K3, p25, k3; turn.
Repeat Rows 3-4 another 13 times = 31 sts and 30 rows.

Turn heel:
Row 1 (RS): K18, ssk, k1, turn.
Row 2 (WS): Sl 1, p6, p2 tog, p1, turn.
Row 3: Sl 1 pwise, knit until 1 st before the gap, ssk, k1, turn.
Row 4: Sl 1pwise, purl until 1 st before the gap, p 2tog, p1, turn.
Repeat rows 3 and 4 another 4 times, until decreases are complete on both sides of the needle and 19 heel sts remain.

GUSSET
Rnd 1:
Ndl 1: Knit 19 sts on heel and then pick up and knit 15 sts along side of heel flap.
Ndls 2 and 3: Work across in instep pattern following chart.
Ndl 4: Pick up and knit 15 sts along heel flap, k9 from ndl 1.

Rnd 2:

Ndl 1: K25.

Ndls 2 and 3: Continue in rhombus pattern over instep sts.

Ndl 4: K24.

(25+16+17+24 sts)

Rnd 3:

Ndl 1: Knit until 3 sts remain and end with k2tog, k1.

Ndls 2 and 3: Continue in rhombus pattern.

Ndl 4: K1, ssk, knit to end of ndl.

Rnds 4-5:

Ndl 1: Knit.

Ndls 2 and 3: Continue in rhombus pattern.

Ndl 4: Knit.

Repeat Rnds 3-5 another 7 times.

(17+16+17+16 sts)

FOOT

Nd. 1: K17.

Ndls 2 and 3: Work across in rhombus instep pattern.

Nd. 4: K16.

Continue in pattern as set until foot is 2 in (5 cm) less than total foot length (see Table). If possible, end the instep pattern either on Row 18 or 36.

BAND TOE

Knit 2 rnds.

Shaping

Ndl 1: Knit to last 3 sts on ndl and end with k2tog, k1.

Ndl 2: K1, ssk, knit remaining sts.

Ndl 3: Work as for ndl 1.

Ndl 4: Work as for ndl 2.

Knit 3 rnds and decrease on Rnd 4.

(Knit 2 rnds and dec on Rnd 3) 2 times.

Knit 1 rnd and dec on rnd 2) 4 times

Decrease on each of the next 6 rnds.

FINISHING

Cut yarn and thread end onto tapestry needle. Pull end through remaining 10 sts. Pull tight and then weave in all ends neatly on WS.

Make the second sock the same way.

Shoe size: U.S. (Euro)	5-6 (36)	6-7 (37)	7-8 (38)	8-9 (39)	9-10 (40)	10-11 (41)	11-12 (42)
Foot length	9 ½ in	9 ½ in	9 ½-9 ¾ in	10 in	10 ¼ in	10 ½-10 ¾ in	10 ¾ in
	(23.5 cm)	(24 cm)	(24.5-25 cm)	(25.5 cm)	(26 cm)	(26.5-27 cm)	(27.5 cm)
Sock length heel to toe	7 ¼ in	7 ½ in	7 ¾-8 in	8 in	8 ¼ in in	8 ½-8 ¾ in	8 ¾ in
	(18.5 cm)	(19 cm)	(19.5-20 cm)	(20.5 cm)	(21 cm)	(21.5-22 cm)	(22.5 cm)

Summer Meadow

Wherever you look, splendorous fields of wildflowers unfold. Little blossoms peek out from blades of grass, inviting you to a picnic—a welcome escape from our hectic lives.

Summer Meadow

LEVEL OF DIFFICULTY
Intermediate

SIZES
Women's U.S. 5-6, 6-7, 7-8, 8-9, 9-10, 10-11, 11-12 (European 36, 37, 38, 39, 40, 41, 42)

Leg circumference: 8 ¾-11 in (22-28 cm)

Foot circumference: 8 ¼-9 ¾ in (21-25 cm)

The length of the sock can be determined by using the respective shoe size.

MATERIALS
Yarn: Fingering (CYCA #1), Regia 4-ply (75% wool/25% nylon; 229 yd/50 g), Cherry (#2002) and Fern (#1092), 50 g each

Needles: 2 circular needles U.S. size 0 or 1.5 (2 or 2.5 mm) or size needed to obtain gauge

Crochet hook: U.S. A-B (2 mm)

Tapestry needle

GAUGE
30 sts and 42 rows in stockinette = 4 x 4 in (10 x 10 cm)

33 sts and 42 rows in leg pattern = 4 x 4 in (10 x 10 cm)

KNITTING BOOKLET
Chart, p. 6

TECHNIQUES
Right- and left-leaning decreases, p. 109

Wrap and Turn (w&t), pp. 110-111

Two-color stranded knitting, pp. 112-113

Toe-up Construction, p. 114

RIBBING
K1tbl, p1; rep from * to *.

LEG AND INSTEP PATTERN
See Booklet, p. 6.

INSTRUCTIONS

Toe-up Construction
With Natural, CO 13 sts onto one circular for the sole and CO 12 sts onto second circular for the instep.
Ndl 1: K12, slip 1 st off ndl.
Ndl 2: K12.
(12+12 sts)

Increases:
At the beginning of each ndl, k2, M1R, knit to last 2 sts, M1L, k2. Knit 1 rnd.
Repeat these 2 rnds 2 more times.

Work 1 increase rnd, knit 2 rnds.
Repeat these 3 rnds 3 more times.

Work 1 increase rnd, knit 3 rnds.
Repeat these 4 rnds 1 more time.
(30+30 sts)

Now begin pattern:
Ndl 1: Work 30 sts in instep pattern.
Ndl 2: Work as for ndl 1.

Continue in pattern until foot is 2 in (5 cm) less than total foot length (see Table).

HEEL

With Natural, work the heel in short rows only across the sts of needle 1.

Row 1 (RS): K29, w&t.

Row 2 (WS): P28, w&t.

Row 3: Knit to 1 st before the next wrapped st, w&t.

Row 4: Purl to 1 st before the next wrapped st, w&t.

Repeat Rows 3 and 4 another 8 times. There should now be 10 wrapped sts on each side and 10 unwrapped knit sts in the center of the needle.

Row 21: K10, knit next st with its wrap, w&t.

Row 22: P11, purl next st with its wrap, w&t.

Row 23: Knit to next wrapped st and then knit next st with its wrap, w&t.

Row 24: Purl to next wrapped st and then purl next st with its wrap, w&t.

Repeat Rows 23-24 another 8 times. Every wrapped st should now be joined with its wrap. (30+30 sts)

LEG

Ndl 1: Work 30 sts in Leg pattern.

Ndl 2: Work as for Ndl 1.

Continue in pattern for 2 in (5 cm).

RIBBING

Work 10 rnds in k1tbl, p1 rib.

BO all sts. Slip the last st onto the crochet hook and work the picot edging along bind-off row: *Ch 3, sl st into first st of chain, skip 2 sts on bind-off row, sc into next st; rep from * around.

FINISHING

Weave in all ends neatly on WS.

Make the second sock the same way.

Shoe size: U.S. (Euro)	5-6 (36)	6-7 (37)	7-8 (38)	8-9 (39)	9-10 (40)	10-11 (41)	11-12 (42)
Foot length	9 ½ in	9 ½ in	9 ½-9 ¾ in	10 in	10 ¼ in	10 ½-10 ¾ in	10 ¾ in
	(23.5 cm)	(24 cm)	(24.5-25 cm)	(25.5 cm)	(26 cm)	(26.5-27 cm)	(27.5 cm)
Sock length heel to toe	7 ¼ in	7 ½ in	7 ¾-8 in	8 in	8 ¼ in in	8 ½-8 ¾ in	8 ¾ in
	(18.5 cm)	(19 cm)	(19.5-20 cm)	(20.5 cm)	(21 cm)	(21.5-22 cm)	(22.5 cm)

Fall Sampler

Summer warmth is losing ground to cooler
temperatures. This filigree pattern sports
the same rich browns peeking out from
behind the silver-grey bark of birch trees
in fall.

Fall Sampler

LEVEL OF DIFFICULTY
Intermediate

SIZES
Women's: U.S. 5-6, 6-7, 7-8, 8-9, 9-10, 10-11, 11-12 (European 36, 37, 38, 39, 40, 41, 42)

Leg circumference: 8 ¼-10 ¾ in (21-27 cm)

Foot circumference: 8-9 ½ in (20-24 cm)

Men's: U.S. 8 ½, 9, 10 ½, 11 ½ (European 42, 43, 44, 45)

Leg circumference: 9 -11 ½ in (23-29 cm)

Foot circumference: 9-10 ¼ in (23-26 cm)

The length of the sock can be determined by using the respective shoe size.

Instructions and stitch counts in parentheses or after a slash refer to Men's sizes.

MATERIALS
Yarn: Fingering (CYCA #1), Regia 4-ply (75% wool/25% nylon; 229 yd/50 g), Tan (#2070) 100 g; Brown (#2140) and Mocha (#2905), 50 g each

Needles: 2 circulars U.S. size 0 or 1.5 (2 or 2.5 mm)

Tapestry needle

GAUGE
30 sts and 42 rows in stockinette = 4 x 4 x in (10 x 10 cm)

33 sts and 40 rows in two-color stranded knitting = 4 x 4 in (10 x 10 cm)

KNITTING BOOKLET
Chart, p. 4

TECHNIQUES
Two-color stranded
 knitting, pp. 112-113

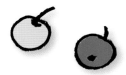

RIBBING
*K3, p1; rep from * around.

LEG PATTERN
See Booklet, p. 4.

INSTRUCTIONS

With Wood, CO 68 sts and divide onto 2 circulars with 34 sts each (CO 72 sts and divide onto 2 circulars with 36 sts each). Join to work in the round, being careful not to twist cast-on row. With Wood, work 12 rnds in k3, p1 ribbing.

LEG
Work 40 rnds in leg pattern. Next, work 2 rnds with Wood.
(34+34 sts/36+36 sts)

Shaping:
Ndl 1: With Wood, *k15 (16), k2tog; rep from * once more.
Ndl 2: Work as for ndl 1.
(32+32/34+34 sts)

Continue with Wood only.
Continue on leg in stockinette until leg is a total of 6 ¼ in (16 cm) long.

HEEL
Work the heel back and forth over the sts on ndl 1. Set sts on ndls 2 aside to be worked later for instep.

Row 1:
Ndl 1: K32 (34); turn.

Row 2:
Ndl 1: K1, p30 (32), k1; turn.

Repeat Rows 1-2 another 13 (15) times. The heel has a total of 32 (34) sts and 28 (32) rows.

Turn heel:
Row 1 (RS): K17 (19), ssk, k1; turn.
Row 2 (WS): Sl 1 pwise, p3 (5), p2tog, p1; turn.
Row 3: Sl 1 pwise, knit until 1 st before the gap, ssk, k1; turn.
Row 4: Sl 1 pwise, purl until 1 st before the gap, p2tog, p1; turn.
Repeat Rows 3-4 another 5 times.
(18 /20 heel sts)

GUSSET (WORK IN THE ROUND)
Rnd 1:
Ndl 1: K18 (20), pick up and knit 14 (16) sts along side of heel flap.
Ndl 2: Knit.

Rnd 2:

Ndl 1: Pick up and knit 14 (16) sts along side of heel flap, k32 (36).

Ndl 2: Knit.

(46+32/53+34) sts

Rnd 3:

Ndls 1 and 2: Knit.

Rnd 4:

Ndl 1: K1, ssk, knit to last 3 sts on ndl and end with k2tog, k1.

Ndl 2: Knit.

Rnds 5-6:

Ndls 1 and 2: Knit.

Rep Rnds 4-6 another 6 (8) times.

(32+32/34+34 sts)

For Women's sizes 5-8 (36-38), the width of the foot should be decreased. On the 4th round , decrease on both ndls 1 and 2.

(Sizes 5-8/36-38: 30+30 sts)

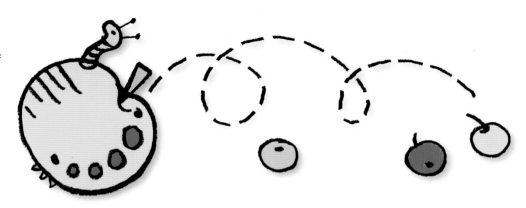

FOOT

Continue in stockinette until foot is desired length from heel to toe (see Table).

BAND TOE

Knit 2 rnds.

Shaping

Nd l 1: K1, ssk, knit to last 3 sts on ndl and end with k2tog, k1.

Ndl 2: Work as for ndl 1.

Knit 3 rnds and decrease on Rnd 4.

(Knit 2 rnds and dec on Rnd 3) 3 times.

Knit 1 rnd and dec on rnd 2) 4 times

Decrease on each of the next 5 (6) rnds except for sizes U.S. 5-8 (36-38), decease on next 4 rnds.

FINISHING

Cut yarn and thread end onto tapestry needle. Pull end through remaining 8 sts. Pull tight and then weave in all ends neatly on WS.

Make the second sock the same way.

Shoe size: U.S. (Euro)	5-6 (36)	6-7 (37)	7-8 (38)	8-9 (39)	9-10 (40)	10-11 (41)	11-12 (42)	Men's 9 (43)	Men's 10 ½ (44)	Men's 11 ½ (45)
Foot length	9 ½ in	9 ½ in	9 ½-9 ¾ in	10 in	10 ¼ in	10 ½-10 ¾ in	10 ¾ in	11 in	11 ¼-11 ½ in	11 ½ in
	(23.5 cm)	(24 cm)	(24.5-25 cm)	(25.5 cm)	(26 cm)	(26.5-27 cm)	(27.5 cm)	(28 cm)	(28.5-29 cm)	(29.5 cm)
Sock length heel to toe	7 ¼ in	7 ½ in	7 ¾-8 in	8 in	8 ¼ in in	8 ½-8 ¾ in	8 ¾ in	8 ¾ in	9-9 ¼ in	9 ½ in
	(18.5 cm)	(19 cm)	(19.5-20 cm)	(20.5 cm)	(21 cm)	(21.5-22 cm)	(22.5 cm)	(22.5 cm)	(23-23.5 cm)	(24.5 cm)

Fall Bouquet

In the fall, nature pulls out all the stops. Everything is blooming in vibrant colors! You don't even need a green thumb to create this beautiful bouquet.

Fall Bouquet

LEVEL OF DIFFICULTY
Experienced

SIZES
Women's U.S. 5-6, 6-7, 7-8, 8-9, 9-10, 10-11, 11-12 (European 36, 37, 38, 39, 40, 41, 42)

Leg circumference: 8 ¼ -10 ¾ in (21-27 cm)

Foot circumference: 8-9 ½ in (20-24 cm)

The length of the sock can be determined by using the respective shoe size.

MATERIALS
Yarn: Fingering (CYCA #1), Regia 4-ply (75% wool/25% nylon; 229 yd/50 g), Burgundy (#0315) and Cherry (#2002), 100 g each; Pine (# 0327), 50 g

Needles: 2 circular needles U.S. size 0 or 1.5 (2 or 2.5 mm) or size needed to obtain gauge

Tapestry needle

GAUGE
30 sts and 42 rows in stockinette = 4 x 4 in (10 x 10 cm)

35 sts and 40 rows in two-color stranded knitting = 4 x 4 in (10 x 10 cm)

KNITTING BOOKLET
Chart, p. 9

TECHNIQUES
Wrap and turn (w&t), pp. 110-111

Two-color stranded knitting, pp. 112-113

Right- and left-leaning decreases, p. 109

CUFF PATTERN
Rnds 1-3: *K2 with Burgundy, p2 with Cherry*; rep from * 17 more times.
Rnd 4: *K2 with Burgundy, p2 with Pine*; rep from * 17 more times.

FLOWER PATTERN
See Booklet, p. 9.

INSTRUCTIONS

With Burgundy, CO 72 sts and divide onto 2 circulars with 36 sts on each ndl. Join, being careful not to twist cast-on row.
(36+36 sts)

Knit 12 rnds and then work 15 rnds in Cuff pattern (3 x Rnds 1-4 and then 1 x Rnds 1-3).

LEG
With Pine, knit 1 rnd.

Shaping:
Ndl 1: With Pine, p2tog, p34.
Ndl 2: Work as for ndl 1.
(35+35 sts)

Work 56 rnds in Flower pattern following chart.

HEEL

The heel is worked with Burgundy only on short rows over the sts on ndl 1:

Row 1 (RS): K34, w&t.

Row 2 (WS): P33, w&t.

Row 3: Knit until 1 st before the next unwrapped st, w&t.

Row 4: Purl until 1 st before the next unwrapped st, w&t.

Rep Rows 3-4 another 9 times until there are 11 wrapped sts on each side of the center 13 unwrapped sts.

Row 23: K13, knit next st with its wrap, w&t.

Row 24: P14, purl next st with its wrap, w&t.

Row 25: Knit to next wrapped st, knit the wrapped st with its wrap, w&t.

Row 26: Purl to next wrapped st, purl the wrapped st with its wrap, w&t.

Rep Rows 25-26 another 9 times — only the two outermost wrapped sts remain.

FOOT

The foot is worked around in multi-color pattern: work 56 rnds in Flower pattern.

Cut Cherry and continue only with Burgundy until foot is 2 in (5 cm) less than total foot length (see Table).

BAND TOE

Knit 1 rnd.

With ndls 1 and 2: *K5, k2tog; rep from * another 9 times.

Knit 1 rnd.

(30+30 sts)

Shaping:

Ndl 1: K1, ssk, knit until 3 sts rem and end with k2tog, k1.

Ndl 2: Work as for ndl 1.

Knit 3 rnds and then work 1 decrease rnd.

Knit 1 rnd with Cherry and then knit 1 rnd with Pine.

Work 1 decrease rnd with Cherry. Cut Cherry and Pine.

Continue in stockinette with Burgundy and shape as follows:

Knit 2 rnds and dec on Rnd 3.

Knit 1 rnd and dec on rnd 2) 4 times

Decrease on each of the next 5 rnds.

FINISHING

Cut yarn and thread end onto tapestry needle. Pull end through remaining 8 sts. Pull tight and then weave in all ends neatly on WS.

Make the second sock the same way.

Shoe size: U.S. (Euro)	5-6 (36)	6-7 (37)	7-8 (38)	8-9 (39)	9-10 (40)	10-11 (41)	11-12 (42)
Foot length	9 ½ in	9 ½ in	9 ½-9 ¾ in	10 in	10 ¼ in	10 ½-10 ¾ in	10 ¾ in
	(23.5 cm)	(24 cm)	(24.5-25 cm)	(25.5 cm)	(26 cm)	(26.5-27 cm)	(27.5 cm)
Sock length heel to toe	7 ¼ in	7 ½ in	7 ¾-8 in	8 in	8 ¼ in in	8 ½-8 ¾ in	8 ¾ in
	(18.5 cm)	(19 cm)	(19.5-20 cm)	(20.5 cm)	(21 cm)	(21.5-22 cm)	(22.5 cm)

Greetings from the High North

A tone-on-tone effect in natural colors rings in the colder season. The two-color Norwegian-style pattern portrays the image of snowflakes. It's such a shame to hide them in boots!

Greetings from the High North

LEVEL OF DIFFICULTY
Experienced

SIZES
Women's U.S. 7-8, 8-9, 9-10, 10-11, 11-12 (European 38, 39, 40, 41, 42)

Leg circumference: 8 ¾-11 in (22-28 cm)

Foot circumference: 8 ¼-9 ¾ in (21-25 cm)

The length of the sock can be determined by using the respective shoe size.

MATERIALS
Yarn: Fingering (CYCA #1), Regia 4-ply (75% wool/25% nylon; 229 yd/50 g), Charcoal (#0522), 100 g; Flannel gray (#0033) and Natural (#1992), 50 g each

Needles: 2 circular needles U.S. size 0 or 1.5 (2 or 2.5 mm) or size needed to obtain gauge

Tapestry needle

GAUGE
30 sts and 40 rows in stockinette = 4 x 4 in (10 x 10 cm).

35 sts and 40 rows in two-color stranded knitting = 4 x 4 in (10 x 10 cm)

KNITTING BOOKLET
Charts, p. 10

TECHNIQUES
Two-color stranded knitting, pp. 112-113

Right- and left-leaning deceases, p. 109

The "gap" on heel turn, p. 111

RIBBING
*K1tbl, p1; rep from * around.

HEEL PATTERN
RS: K1, *k1, sl 1 pwise; rep from * 15 more times, end with k2.
WS: K1, p33, k1.

LEG, INSTEP, SOLE PATTERN, SOLE PATTERN WITH GUSSET SHAPING
See Booklet, p. 10.

INSTRUCTIONS

With Charcoal, CO 72 sts and divide onto 2 circulars, with 36 sts on each ndl. Join, being careful not to twist cast-on row.
Work 4 rnds in ribbing.

LEG
Work 54 rnds in leg pattern (3 x Rnds 1-18). (36+36 sts)

HEEL
Set-up heel by slipping the last st on ndl 1 to ndl 2 (35+37 sts). Cut Natural and Flannel.
Work 32 rows in heel pattern back and forth over sts on ndl 1 with Charcoal.

Turn heel:
Row 1 (RS): K18, ssk, k1; turn.
Row 2 WS): Sl 1 pwise, p2, p2tog, p1; turn.
Row 3: Sl 1 pwise, knit until 1 st before the gap, ssk, k1; turn.
Row 4: Sl 1 pwise, purl until 1 st before the gap, p2tog, p1; turn.
Repeat Rows 3-4 another 6 times; cut yarn. (19 heel sts)

GUSSET
With ndl 1 and Charcoal, pick up and knit 16 sts along right side of heel flap, k19 heel sts, pick up and knit 16 along left side of heel flap.

Rnd 1:

Ndl 2: Work in instep pattern.

Ndl 1: Work in sole pattern, shaping gusset at the same time (see chart).

Rnd 2:

Ndl 2: Work in instep pattern.

Ndl 1: Work in sole pattern, shaping gusset at the same time.

Work 25 Rnds in gusset pattern (Rnds 1-2) until all the gusset decreases have been worked and 35 sts rem on ndl 1.

FOOT

Ndl 2: Work 37 sts in instep pattern.

Ndl 1: Work 35 sts in sole pattern.

Continue in foot pattern as set until foot is desired length from heel to toe (see Table).

BAND TOE

Cut Flannel and Natural and continue with Charcoal only.

Knit 1 rnd, slipping the first st on ndl 2 to ndl 1. (36+36 sts)

Ndl 2: *K4, k2tog; rep from * 5 more times.

Ndl 1: Work as for ndl 2.

(30+30 sts)

Knit 1 rnd.

Shaping:

Ndl 2: K1, ssk, knit until 3 sts rem on ndl and end with k2tog, k1.

Ndl 1: Work as for ndl 2.

Knit 3 rnds and decrease on Rnd 4.

(Knit 2 rnds and dec on Rnd 3) 2 times.

Knit 1 rnd and dec on rnd 2) 3 times

Decrease on each of the next 6 rnds.

FINISHING

Cut yarn and thread end onto tapestry needle. Pull end through remaining 8 sts. Pull tight and then weave in all ends neatly on WS.

Make the second sock the same way.

Shoe size: U.S. (Euro)	7-8 (38)	8-9 (39)	9-10 (40)	10-11 (41)	11-12 (42)
Foot length	9 ½-9 ¾ in	10 in	10 ¼ in	10 ½-10 ¾ in	10 ¾ in
	(24.5-25 cm)	(25.5 cm)	(26 cm)	(26.5-27 cm)	(27.5 cm)
Sock length heel to toe	7 ¾-8 in	8 in	8 ¼ in in	8 ½-8 ¾ in	8 ¾ in
	(19.5-20 cm)	(20.5 cm)	(21 cm)	(21.5-22 cm)	(22.5 cm)

Climbing Roses

The romantic wooden pergola in an old cottage garden has been whitened by wind and weather. The sun-loving plants are now settling in for winter quiet as summer wanes and the first hint of autumn eases in.

Climbing Roses

LEVEL OF DIFFICULTY
Experienced

SIZES
Women's U.S. 7-8, 8-9, 9-10, 10-11, 11-12 (European 38, 39, 40, 41, 42)

Leg circumference: 8 ¾-10 ¾ in (22-27 cm)

Foot circumference: 8-10 ¼ in (20-26 cm)

The length of the sock can be determined by using the respective shoe size.

MATERIALS
Yarn: Fingering (CYCA #1), Regia 4-ply (75% wool/25% nylon; 229 yd/50 g), Flannel gray (#0033) and Mocha (#2905), 100 g each

Needles: 2 circular needles U.S. size 0 or 1.5 (2 or 2.5 mm) or size needed to obtain gauge

Extra dpn or circular for picking up sts on picot edging

Tapestry needle

GAUGE
30 sts and 42 rows in stockinette = 4 x 4 in (10 x 10 cm)

35 sts and 40 rows in two-color stranded knitting = 4 x 4 in (10 x 10 cm)

KNITTING BOOKLET
Charts, pp. 12-13

TECHNIQUES
Right- and left-leaning deceases, p. 109

Make 1 (M1) increase, p. 108

Wrap and Turn (w&t), pp. 110-111

Two-color stranded knitting, pp. 112-113

RIBBING
*K1tbl, p1; rep from * around.

LEG, INSTEP, FRONT OF FOOT PATTERNS
See Booklet, pp. 12-13.

INSTRUCTIONS

With Flannel, CO 76 sts and divide onto 2 circulars with 38 sts on each ndl. Join, being careful not to twist cast-on row.
(38+38 sts)
Knit 8 rnds in St st.
Next rnd (holes): *K2tog, yo; rep from * another 37 times.
Knit 9 rounds.

To form the picot edge which is folded at the lace row, * with the extra ndl and, working on WS, pick up 38 loops from cast-on row, making sure that picked up sts are directly below live sts. Place ndl with picked up loops behind ndl 1 and then join the sets of sts together with k2tog around. Rep from * with the 38 sts on ndl 2.

Work 12 rnds in k1tbl, p1 ribbing.

LEG
Knit 2 rnds in St st.
Work 41 rnds in Rose pattern following the chart. For the left sock, read the chart from right to left. For a right sock that is mirror-image of the left, read the chart from left to right.
(38+38 sts)

HEEL
Cut Mocha.
The heel is worked with Flannel only, in short rows with the sts on ndl 2. After working Rnd 41 of the Rose pattern over the sts on ndl 2; turn.

Set-up Row (WS):
Ndl 2: Sl 1 pwise, p37, p21 sts from ndl 1; turn.

Row 1 (RS): Sl 1 pwise, k3, *k2tog, k7; rep from * another 2 times, k2tog, k4, w&t.
Slip the rem 21 sts on ndl 2 to ndl 1.
(38+34 sts)

Row 2 (WS): Sl 1 pwise, p32; w&t.
Row 3: Knit until 1 st before the next unwrapped st; w&t.
Row 4: Purl until 1 st before the next unwrapped st; w&t.
Rep Rows 3-4 another 9 times. There should be 11 wrapped sts on each side of the center 12 unwrapped sts.

Shoe size: U.S. (Euro)	7-8 (38)	8-9 (39)	9-10 (40)	10-11 (41)	11-12 (42)
Foot length	9 ½-9 ¾ in	10 in	10 ¼ in	10 ½-10 ¾ in	10 ¾ in
	(24.5-25 cm)	(25.5 cm)	(26 cm)	(26.5-27 cm)	(27.5 cm)
Sock length heel to toe	7 ¾-8 in	8 in	8 ¼ in in	8 ½-8 ¾ in	8 ¾ in
	(19.5-20 cm)	(20.5 cm)	(21 cm)	(21.5-22 cm)	(22.5 cm)

Row 23: K12, knit the next st with its wrap; w&t.

Row 24: P13, purl the next st with its wrap; w&t.

Row 25: Knit to the next wrapped st, knit wrapped st tog with its 2 wraps; w&t.

Row 26: Purl to the next wrapped st, purl wrapped st tog with its 2 wraps; w&t.

Rep Rows 25-26 another 9 times until only the two outermost wrapped sts remain.
(38+34 sts)

FOOT

Set-up Row (RS):

Ndl 2: K5, M1, *k8, M1; rep from * another 2 times, k5.
(38+38 sts)

Work 53 rnds in instep pattern.
(35+37 sts)

Work foot pattern until foot is 2 in (5 cm) less than total foot length (see Table).

Cut Mocha.

Slip the first st on ndl 2 to ndl 1.
(36+36 sts)

Band Toe

The toe is worked only with Flannel.

Knit 1 rnd.

Ndls 1 and 2: *K7, k2tog; rep another 7 times.
(32+32 sts)

Knit 2 rnds.

Shaping:

Ndl 1: K1, ssk, knit until 3 sts rem on ndl and end with k2tog, k1.

Ndl 2: Work as for ndl 1.

Knit 3 rnds and decrease on Rnd 4.

(Knit 2 rnds and dec on Rnd 3) 2 times.

Knit 1 rnd and dec on rnd 2) 4 times

Decrease on each of the next 6 rnds.

FINISHING

Cut yarn and thread end onto tapestry needle.

Pull end through remaining 8 sts. Pull tight and then weave in all ends neatly on WS.

Make the second sock the same way.

Violett & Co.

Ah Heather! When the moors are blooming, fall is near. A simple walk becomes a colorful experience. Dark blue and purple dominate this pallet. These socks will keep the feet of any outdoor enthusiast warm and cozy.

Violett & Co.

LEVEL OF DIFFICULTY
Intermediate

SIZES
Men's: U.S. 8 ½, 9, 10 ½, 11 ½ (European 42, 43, 44, 45)

Leg circumference: 9-11 ½ in (23-29 cm)

Foot circumference: 8 ¾-10 ¼ in (22-26 cm)

The length of the sock can be determined by using the respective shoe size.

MATERIALS
Yarn: Fingering (CYCA #1), Trekking Edition Understatement (75% wool/25% nylon; 459 yd/100 g), Blue/Purple (#322), 100 g

Needles: Set of 5 dpn U.S. size 0 or 1.5 (2 or 2.5 mm) or size needed to obtain gauge

Cable needle

Tapestry needle

GAUGE
32 sts and 42 rows in stockinette = 4 x 4 in (10 x 10 cm).

35 sts and 40 rows in cable pattern = 4 x 4 in (10 x 10 cm).

KNITTING BOOKLET
Charts, p. 14

TECHNIQUES
Right- and left-leaning deceases, p. 109

The "gap" on heel turn, p. 111

RIBBING
See Booklet, p. 14.

LEG AND INSTEP PATTERNS, CABLES
See Booklet, p. 14.

INSTRUCTIONS

CO 72 sts and divide evenly onto 4 dpn with 18 sts on each ndl. Join, being careful not to twist cast-on row. Work 16 rnds in charted cuff pattern (4 x Rnds 1-4).

LEG
Continue in leg pattern; there should be 1 rep of 18 sts on each dpn.

Adjust the cable sts at needle changes as follows: Rnds 6 and 30: With ndl 4, knit the 1st st on ndl 1. Begin Rnd 7 (31) on ndl 1. On Rnds 7 (31), work the 1st st on each ndl with the previous ndl, shifting sts.

Rnds 21 and 33: The last st on ndl 4 is on the cable ndl behind the work and is worked with the first cable on Rnds 22 (34).

Work 54 rnds in pattern (1 x Rnds 1-36 and 1 x Rnds 1-18).

(18+18+18+18 sts)

On the last rnd, slip the last 2 sts on ndl 4 to ndl 1; turn.

(20+18+18+16 sts)

HEEL
Move the sts on ndls 4 and 3 onto one dpn. The heel is worked back and forth over 34 sts.

Row 1 (WS): K3, p13, p2tog, p13, k3; turn (33 heel sts).

Row 2 (RS): K3, *sl 1 pwise, k1; rep from * another 12 times, sl 1, k3; turn.

Row 3: K3, p27, k3; turn.

Rep Rows 2-3 another 14 times.

Turn heel:

Row 1 (RS): K18, ssk, k1; turn.

Row 2 WS): Sl 1 pwise, p4, p2tog, p1; turn.

Row 3: Sl 1 pwise, knit until 1 st before the gap, ssk, k1; turn.

Row 4: Sl 1 pwise, purl until 1 st before the gap, p2tog, p1; turn.

Repeat Rows 3-4 another 5 times; cut yarn.

(19 heel sts)

GUSSET

Rnd 1:

Ndl 4: K19 heel sts, pick up and knit 16 along side of heel flap.

Ndls 1 and 2: Work Rnd 1 of instep pattern.

Ndl 3: Pick up and knit 15 sts along side of heel flap, k10 from ndl 4.

Ndl 4: K25.

Rnd 2:

Ndls 1 and 2: Work in instep pattern.

Ndls 3 and 4: K25.

(19+19+25+25 sts)

Rnd 3: Ndls 1 and 2: Work in instep pattern.

Ndl 3: K1, ssk, knit rem sts on ndl.

Ndl 4: Knit until 3 sts rem on ndl and end with k2tog, k1.

Rnds 4-5:

Ndls 1 and 2: Work in instep pattern.

Ndls 3-4: Knit.

Repeat Rows 3-5 another 7 times.

(19+19+17+17 sts)

FOOT

Ndls 1 and 2: Work in instep pattern.

Ndls 3 and 4: Knit.

Continue as set until foot is 2 in (5 cm) less than total foot length (see Table).

BAND TOE

Transition row:

Ndl 1: Work 2 sts in cable pattern for the toe band, p1 and knit rem sts on ndl.

Ndl 2: Knit to the last 3 sts on ndl and end with p1, 2 sts in cable pattern for toe band.

Ndl 3: P1, knit rem sts on ndl.

Ndl 4: Knit to the last st and end with p1.

Work the transition rnd two times.

(19+19+17+17 sts)

Shaping:

Ndl 1: Work 2 sts in cable pattern for the toe band, p1, ssk, knit to end of ndl.

Ndl 2: Knit to last 5 sts and end with k2tog, p1, 2 sts in cable pattern for toe band.

Ndl 3: P1, ssk, knit to end of ndl.

Ndl 4: Knit to last 3 sts and end with k2tog, p1.

Continue in pattern as set, shaping as follows:

Knit 3 rnds and decrease on Rnd 4.

(Knit 2 rnds and dec on Rnd 3) 2 times.

Knit 1 rnd and dec on rnd 2) 4 times

Decrease on each of the next 8 rnds.

FINISHING

Cut yarn and thread end onto tapestry needle. Pull end through remaining 8 sts. Pull tight and then weave in all ends neatly on WS.

Make the second sock the same way.

Shoe size: U.S. (Euro)	Men's 8 ½ 11-12 (42)	Men's 9 (43)	Men's 10 ½ (44)	Men's 11 ½ (45)
Foot length	10 ¾ in	11 in	11 ¼-11 ½ in	11 ½ in
	(27.5 cm)	(28 cm)	(28.5-29 cm)	(29.5 cm)
Sock length heel to toe	8 ¾ in	8 ¾ in	9-9 ¼ in	9 ½ in
	(22.5 cm)	(22.5 cm)	(23-23.5 cm)	(24.5 cm)

Inspirations

Grey patches of fog hang over the fields. A tree and its bare branches are hidden by the early morning mist and then glisten in the first light of day: these fall impressions are captured in a heathery grey-brown yarn.

Inspirations

LEVEL OF DIFFICULTY
Experienced

SIZES
Women's U.S. 5-6, 6-7, 7-8, 8-9, 9-10, 10-11, 11-12 (European 36, 37, 38, 39, 40, 41, 42)

Leg circumference: 8 ¼-10 ¾ in (21-27 cm)

Foot circumference: 8-9 ½ in (20-24 cm)

The length of the sock can be determined by using the respective shoe size.

MATERIALS
Yarn: Fingering (CYCA #1), Regia 4-ply (75% wool/25% nylon; 229 yd/50 g), Tan (#2070), 100 g

Needles: 2 circular needles U.S. size 0 or 1.5 (2 or 2.5 mm) or size needed to obtain gauge

Cable needle

Tapestry needle

GAUGE
32 sts and 42 rows in stockinette = 4 x 4 in (10 x 10 cm)

35 sts and 40 rows in cable pattern = 4 x 4 in (10 x 10 cm)

KNITTING BOOKLET
Charts, p. 11

TECHNIQUES
Make 1 (M1) increase, p. 108

Right and left decreases, p. 109

The "gap" on heel turn, p. 111

RIBBING
*K3, p2, k2, p2, k3; rep from * around.

HEEL PATTERN
Row 1 (RS): K1, *k1, sl 1 pwise; rep from * another 15 times, k2.
Row 2 (WS): K1, p33, k1.

LEG AND INSTEP PATTERNS
See Booklet, p. 11.

INSTRUCTIONS

CO 60 sts and divide evenly onto 2 circulars with 30 sts on each ndl. Join, being careful not to twist cast-on row.
Work 15 rnds in ribbing.

Transition to Leg pattern:
Ndl 1: *K2, M1, k1, p2, k2, p2, k1, M1, k2; rep from * across ndl.
Ndl 2: Work as for ndl 1.
(35+35 sts)

LEG

Ndls 1 and 2: Work 72 rnds in leg pattern (2 x Rnds 1-36).
(35+35 sts)

HEEL

Work 32 rows back and forth in heel pattern over the 35 sts on ndl 1.

Turn heel:
Row 1 (RS): K20, ssk, k1; turn.
Row 2 (WS): Sl 1 pwise, p6, p2tog, p1; turn.
Row 3: Sl 1 pwise, knit until 1 st before the gap, ssk, k1; turn.
Row 4: Sl 1 pwise, purl until 1 st before the gap, p2tog, p1; turn.
Repeat Rows 3-4 another 5 times (21 heel sts)

GUSSET

Rnd 1:
Ndl 1: Knit 21 heel sts, pick up and knit 16 along side of heel flap.
Ndl 2: Work in instep pattern.

Rnd 2:
Ndl 1: Pick up and knit 16 along side of heel flap, k37.
Ndl 2: Work in instep pattern.
(53+35 sts)

Rnd 3:
Ndl 1: K1, ssk, knit to last 3 sts, and end k2tog, k1.
Ndl 2: Work in instep pattern.

Rnds 4-5:
Ndl 1: Knit.
Ndl 2: Work in instep pattern.

Repeat Rnds 3-5 another 10 times (31+35 sts).

FOOT

Ndl 1: Knit.
Ndl 2: Work in Instep pattern.
Continue as set until foot is 2 in (5 cm) less than total foot length (see Table).

Set-up rnd for toe: Knit around.

Shaping:
Ndl 1: Knit.
Ndl 2: *K5, k2tog, k6, k2tog; rep from * once more, k5.
Knit 1 more rnd.
(31+31 sts)

BAND TOE

Shaping:
Ndl 1: K1, ssk, knit until 3 sts rem on ndl and end with k2tog, k1.
Ndl 2: Work as for ndl 1.

Knit 3 rnds and decrease on Rnd 4.
(Knit 2 rnds and dec on Rnd 3) 2 times.
Knit 1 rnd and dec on rnd 2) 4 times
Decrease on each of the next 5 rnds.

FINISHING

Cut yarn and thread end onto tapestry needle.
Pull end through remaining 10 sts. Pull tight and then weave in all ends neatly on WS.

Make the second sock the same way.

Shoe size: U.S. (Euro)	5-6 (36)	6-7 (37)	7-8 (38)	8-9 (39)	9-10 (40)	10-11 (41)	11-12 (42)
Foot length	9 ½ in	9 ½ in	9 ½-9 ¾ in	10 in	10 ¼ in	10 ½-10 ¾ in	10 ¾ in
	(23.5 cm)	(24 cm)	(24.5-25 cm)	(25.5 cm)	(26 cm)	(26.5-27 cm)	(27.5 cm)
Sock length heel to toe	7 ¼ in	7 ½ in	7 ¾-8 in	8 in	8 ¼ in in	8 ½-8 ¾ in	8 ¾ in
	(18.5 cm)	(19 cm)	(19.5-20 cm)	(20.5 cm)	(21 cm)	(21.5-22 cm)	(22.5 cm)

Winter Mix

Crystal clear nights, icicles hanging from the rooftops and beautiful ice flowers on the windows are inspiration for new knitting projects as winter takes hold. This sumptuous Fair Isle pattern is the perfect challenge for a long winter evening.

Winter Mix

LEVEL OF DIFFICULTY
Experienced

SIZES
Women's U.S. 7-8, 8-9, 9-10, 10-11, 11-12
(European 38, 39, 40, 41, 42)

Leg circumference: 8 ¼-10 ½ in (21-27 cm)

Foot circumference: 8-9 ½ in (20-24 cm)

The length of the sock can be determined by using the respective shoe size.

MATERIALS
Yarn: Fingering (CYCA #1), Regia 4-ply (75% wool/25% nylon; 229 yd/50 g), Jeans heather (#2137), 100 g; Gray-blue heather (#1980), light Camel (#0017), Royal blue (#2000), Tan (#2070), Natural (#1992), Lavender (#1988), and Cardinal (#1078), 50 g each

Needles: 2 circular needles U.S. size 0 or 1.5 (2 or 2.5 mm) or size needed to obtain gauge

Tapestry needle

GAUGE
32 sts and 42 rows in stockinette = 4 x 4 in (10 x 10 cm)

35 sts and 40 rows in two-color stranded knitting = 4 x 4 in (10 x 10 cm)

KNITTING BOOKLET
Charts, p. 16

TECHNIQUES
Two-color stranded knitting, pp. 112-113

Wrap and Turn (w&t), pp. 110-111

LEG, INSTEP, AND SOLE PATTERNS
See Booklet, p. 16.

INSTRUCTIONS

With Jeans and the 2 circular ndls, CO 72 sts with 36 sts on each needle. Join, being careful not to twist cast-on row. Work around in k2, p2 rib (18 repeats around) in the following color sequence.

Rnds 1-3: *K2 with Jeans, p2 with Natural; rep from * around (18 repeats).

Rnds 4-6: *K2 with Jeans, p2 with light Camel; rep from * around (18 repeats).

Rnd 7-9: *K2 with Jeans, p2 with Wood; rep from * around (18 repeats).

Rnd 10-12 *K2 with Jeans, p2 with Gray-blue; rep from * around (18 repeats).

Now work 46 rnds in two-color stranded knitting following charted pattern for leg. (36+36 sts)

HEEL
Slip the first st on ndl 1 to ndl 2 (35+37 sts).

The heel is worked in short rows on ndl 1 with only one color, Jeans.

Row 1 (RS): K34, w&t.

Row 2 (WS): P33, w&t.

Row 3: Knit to 1 st before the next wrapped st, w&t.

Row 4: Purl to 1 st before the next wrapped st, w&t.

Repeat Rows 3-4 another 10 times. There should now be 12 wrapped sts at each side of the needle and 11 unwrapped sts in the center.

Row 25: K11, knit next st with its wrap, w&t.

Row 26: P12, purl next st with its wrap, w&t.

Row 27: Knit to next wrapped st and then knit next st with its wrap, w&t.

Row 28: Purl to next wrapped st and then purl next st with its wrap, w&t.

Repeat Rows 27-28 another 10 times. Every wrapped st should now be joined with its wrap. (35+37 sts)

Cut all yarns except for Jeans. Reattach yarns as necessary for pattern.

Shoe size: U.S. (Euro)	7-8 (38)	8-9 (39)	9-10 (40)	10-11 (41)	11-12 (42)
Foot length	9 ½-9 ¾ in	10 in	10 ¼ in	10 ½-10 ¾ in	10 ¾ in
	(24.5-25 cm)	(25.5 cm)	(26 cm)	(26.5-27 cm)	(27.5 cm)
Sock length heel to toe	7 ¾-8 in	8 in	8 ¼ in in	8 ½-8 ¾ in	8 ¾ in
	(19.5-20 cm)	(20.5 cm)	(21 cm)	(21.5-22 cm)	(22.5 cm)

FOOT

Now work around on all the stitches, with the sole pattern on ndl 1 and the instep pattern on ndl 2. Work a total of 60 rnds in pattern (2 x Rnds 1-30).

For U.S. sizes 8-9, 9-10, 10-11, 11-12 (Euro 39, 40, 41, 42), after completing pattern, continue in Jeans until foot is desired length to toe.

TOE

Work the toe in Jeans as follows:
Knit 1 rnd. Slip the last st on ndl 2 to ndl 1 (36+36 sts).
Ndls 1 and 2: *K4, k2tog; rep from * 12 times around.
Knit 1 rnd (30+30 sts).

Shaping:
Ndl 1: K1, ssk, knit to last 3 sts on ndl and end k2tog, k1.
Ndl 2: Work as for ndl 1.

Knit 3 rnds and decrease on Rnd 4.
(Knit 2 rnds and dec on Rnd 3) 2 times.
Knit 1 rnd and dec on rnd 2) 3 times
Decrease on each of the next 6 rnds.

FINISHING

Cut yarn and thread end onto tapestry needle. Pull end through remaining 8 sts. Pull tight and then weave in all ends neatly on WS.

Make the second sock the same way.

Winter Flowers

Everyone needs a little mistletoe romance to warm them during this chilly time of year! This classic Nordic design is embellished with red accents in the form of the flowers and berries of the popular winter decoration. Indeed, these hand-knit socks are sure to help heat up your next cold spell.

Winter Flowers

LEVEL OF DIFFICULTY
Intermediate

SIZES
Women's U.S. 5-6, 6-7, 7-8, 8-9, 9-10, 10-11, 11-12 (European 36, 37, 38, 39, 40, 41, 42)

Leg circumference: 8 ¼-10 ¾ in (21-27 cm)

Foot circumference: 8 -9 ½ in (20-24 cm)

The length of the sock can be determined by using the respective shoe size.

MATERIALS
Yarn: Fingering (CYCA #1), Regia 4-ply (75% wool/25% nylon; 229 yd/50 g), Gray-blue heather (#1980), 100 g; Cherry (#2002), Burgundy (#0315), Jeans heather (#2137), and Light Blue (#1945), 50 g each

Needles: 2 circular needles U.S. size 0 or 1.5 (2 or 2.5 mm) or size needed to obtain

Tapestry needle

GAUGE
32 sts and 42 rows in stockinette = 4 x 4 in (10 x 10 cm)

35 sts and 40 rows in two-color stranded knitting = 4 x 4 in (10 x 10 cm)

KNITTING BOOKLET
Chart, p. 18

TECHNIQUES
Right- and left-leaning decreases, p. 109

Make 1 (M1) increase, p. 108

Two-color stranded knitting, pp. 112-113

The "gap" on heel turn, p. 111

RIBBING
K3tbl, p2, k2tbl, p2; rep from * to * around.

LEG PATTERN
See Booklet, p. 18.

INSTRUCTIONS

LEG
With Jeans, CO 72 sts, and divide them evenly onto 2 circulars with 36 sts on each ndl. Join, being careful not to twist cast-on row. Purl 1 rnd and then work 12 rnds in ribbing.
Next, work 46 rnds in charted leg pattern over ndls 1 and 2. (36+36 sts)
Cut all colors but Gray-blue.

Leg Shaping
Ndl 1: With Gray-blue heather, *K7, k2tog; repeat from * 3 more times.
Ndl 2: Work as for ndl 1 (32+32 sts).
Continue with Gray-blue until leg is 7 in (18 cm) long from cast-on row.

HEEL
The heel is worked back and forth in stockinette over the sts on ndl 1. Set sts on ndl 2 aside while you knit heel.
Row 1: K32; turn.
Row 2: K3, p26, k3; turn.
Rep Rows 1-2 another 14 times (32 sts and 30 rows).

Turn heel:
Row 1 (RS): K17, ssk, k1; turn.
Row 2 (WS): Sl 1 pwise, p3, p2tog, p1; turn.
Row 3: Sl 1 pwise, knit until 1 st before the gap, ssk, k1; turn.
Row 4: Sl 1 pwise, purl until 1 st before the gap, p2tog, p1; turn.
Repeat Rows 3-4 another 5 times (18 heel sts remain).

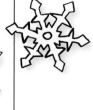

Shoe size: U.S. (Euro)	5-6 (36)	6-7 (37)	7-8 (38)	8-9 (39)	9-10 (40)	10-11 (41)	11-12 (42)
Foot length	9 ½ in	9 ½ in	9 ½-9 ¾ in	10 in	10 ¼ in	10 ½-10 ¾ in	10 ¾ in
	(23.5 cm)	(24 cm)	(24.5-25 cm)	(25.5 cm)	(26 cm)	(26.5-27 cm)	(27.5 cm)
Sock length heel to toe	7 ¼ in	7 ½ in	7 ¾-8 in	8 in	8 ¼ in in	8 ½-8 ¾ in	8 ¾ in
	(18.5 cm)	(19 cm)	(19.5-20 cm)	(20.5 cm)	(21 cm)	(21.5-22 cm)	(22.5 cm)

GUSSET

Rnd 1
Ndl 1: Knit the 18 heel sts, pick up and knit 15 sts along side of heel flap.
Ndl 2: Knit.

Rnd 2
Ndl 1: Pick up and knit 15 sts along other side of heel flap, k33.
Ndl 2: Knit
(48+32 sts)

Rnd 3: Knit around.

Rnd 4:
Ndl 1: K1, ssk, knit to last 3 sts, and end k2tog, k1.
Ndl 2: Knit.

Rnds 5-6: Knit around.

Repeat Rnds 4-6 another 7 times (32+32 sts).

FOOT

Knit around in stockinette over all the sts until foot is 2 in (5 cm) less than desired total foot length (see Table).

BAND TOE

All sizes: Knit 2 rounds.

Shaping:
Ndl 1: K1, ssk, knit to last 3 sts on ndl and end k2tog, k1.
Ndl 2: Work as for ndl 1.

Knit 3 rnds and decrease on Rnd 4.
(Knit 2 rnds and dec on Rnd 3) 2 times.
Knit 1 rnd and dec on rnd 2) 4 times
Decrease on each of the next 6 rnds.

FINISHING

Cut yarn and thread end onto tapestry needle. Pull end through remaining 8 sts. Pull tight and then weave in all ends neatly on WS.

Make the second sock the same way.

Father Frost

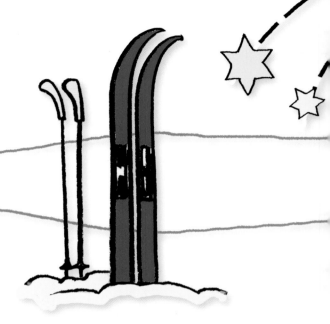

Behold the graceful dance of the Northern lights as the stars ply their paths and brighten the winter sky—these two-colored pattern socks embrace the same delightful contrasts.

Father Frost

LEVEL OF DIFFICULTY
Experienced

SIZES
Women's U.S. 5-6, 6-7, 7-8, 8-9, 9-10, 10-11, 11-12 (European 36, 37, 38, 39, 40, 41, 42)

Leg circumference: 8 ¾ -11 in (22-28 cm)

Foot circumference: 8 -10 ¼ in (20-26 cm)

The length of the sock can be determined by using the respective shoe size.

MATERIALS
Yarn: Fingering (CYCA #1), Regia 4-ply Stretch (70% wool/23% nylon/7% polyester; 219 yd/50 g), Military green (#9996) and Blue jeans (#0054), 100 g each

Needles: 2 circular needles U.S. size 0 or 1.5 (2 or 2.5 mm) or size needed to obtain gauge

Tapestry needle

GAUGE
32 sts and 40 rows in stockinette = 4 x 4 in (10 x 10 cm)

35 sts and 40 rows in two-color stranded knitting = 4 x 4 in (10 x 10 cm)

KNITTING BOOKLET
Charts, pp. 16-17

TECHNIQUES
Right- and left-leaning decreases, p. 109

Two-color stranded knitting, pp. 112-113

TWO-COLOR "RIB"
*K1 with Olive green, k1 with Blue Jeans; repeat from * around.

SOLE PATTERN
*K1 with Blue Jeans, k1 with Olive Green; repeat from * another 16 times and then k1 with Blue Jeans.

LEG, INSTEP, AND HEEL PATTERNS
See Booklet, pp. 16-17.

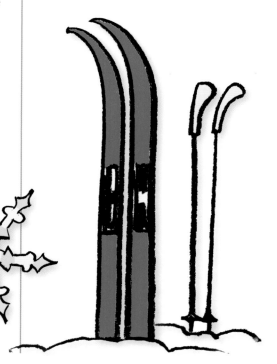

INSTRUCTIONS

With Olive green, CO 70 sts, and divide evenly onto 2 circulars with 35 sts on each ndl. Join, being careful not to twist cast-on row. Knit 10 rnds in stockinette. Work 10 rnds in two-color "rib."

LEG
Ndl 1: Work across in leg and instep pattern for ndl 1 following chart.
Ndl 2: Work across in leg and instep pattern for ndl 2 following chart.
Work 36 rounds in pattern (3 x Rnds 1-12).

HEEL
Work 32 rounds as follows:
Ndl 1: Work in leg and Instep pattern.
Ndl 2: Work in heel pattern.
(35+65 sts).

Turn Heel:
Ndl 1: Work Row 9 of leg and instep pattern.
Ndl 2: Work in short rows as follows:
RS: Work 37 sts of Row 33 of charted heel pattern; turn.
WS: Sl 1 pwise, k7 of Row 34 of heel pattern; turn.
Work through Row 63, slipping the first st after the turn. The last row is a RS row (35+35 sts).

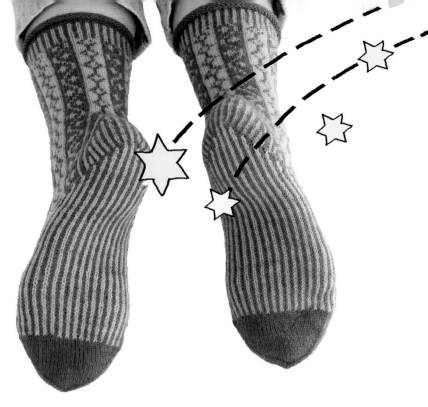

Shaping:

Ndl 1: K1, ssk, knit to last 3 sts on ndl and end k2tog, k1.

Ndl 2: Work as for ndl 1.

Knit 3 rnds and decrease on Rnd 4.

(Knit 2 rnds and dec on Rnd 3) 2 times.

Knit 1 rnd and dec on rnd 2) 3 times

Decrease on each of the next 6 rnds.

FINISHING

Cut yarn and thread end onto tapestry needle. Pull end through remaining 8 sts. Pull tight and then weave in all ends neatly on WS.

Make the second sock the same way.

FOOT

Continue as follows:

Ndl 1: Continue in leg and instep pattern, beginning on Rnd 10.

Ndl 2: Work in sole pattern.

Continue as set until foot is 2 in (5 cm) less than total foot length (see Table).

TOE

Cut Blue Jeans and continue in Olive Green. Knit 1 rnd.

Set-up row for toe shaping:

Ndl 1: *K2tog, k5; repeat from * another 4 times.

Ndl 2: Work as for ndl 1 (30+30 sts).

Knit 1 rnd.

Shoe size: U.S. (Euro)	5-6 (36)	6-7 (37)	7-8 (38)	8-9 (39)	9-10 (40)	10-11 (41)	11-12 (42)
Foot length	9 ½ in	9 ½ in	9 ½-9 ¾ in	10 in	10 ¼ in	10 ½-10 ¾ in	10 ¾ in
	(23.5 cm)	(24 cm)	(24.5-25 cm)	(25.5 cm)	(26 cm)	(26.5-27 cm)	(27.5 cm)
Sock length heel to toe	7 ¼ in	7 ½ in	7 ¾-8 in	8 in	8 ¼ in in	8 ½-8 ¾ in	8 ¾ in
	(18.5 cm)	(19 cm)	(19.5-20 cm)	(20.5 cm)	(21 cm)	(21.5-22 cm)	(22.5 cm)

"Christmassy"

We might dream of a White Christmas, but it's the color red that makes the most impact when winter has sapped the out-of-doors of its natural variation in brilliant shade and hue, leaving a muted palette of dull grays and dusky browns behind. Red noses, a red-clad Santa Claus, the red blooms of the flamboyant Poinsettia—and now these rich red socks worked in traditional Alpine patterns.

"Christmassy"

LEVEL OF DIFFICULTY
Experienced

SIZES
Women's U.S. 6-7, 7-8, 8-9, 9-10, 10-11, 11-12
(European 37, 38, 39, 40, 41, 42)

Leg circumference: 8 ¾-11 in (22-28 cm)

Foot circumference: 8-10 ¼ in (20-26 cm)

The length of the sock can be determined by
using the respective shoe size.

MATERIALS
Yarn: Fingering (CYCA #1), Trekking Uni
(75% wool/25% nylon; 462 yd/100 g),
Red (#1462), 100 g

Needles: 2 circular needles U.S. size 0 or 1.5
(2 or 2.5 mm) or size needed to obtain gauge

Cable needle

2 stitch markers

Tapestry needle

GAUGE
32 sts and 40 rows in stockinette = 4 x 4 in
(10 x 10 cm)

35 sts and 40 rows in cable pattern = 4 x 4 in
(10 x 10 cm)

KNITTING BOOKLET
Charts, pp. 18-19

TECHNIQUES
Make 1 (M1) increase, p. 108

Right- and left-leaning decreases, p. 109

The "gap" heel turn, p. 111

RIBBING
*K1tbl, p1; repeat from * around.

LEG PATTERNS 1 AND 2; HEEL PATTERN
See Booklet, pp. 18-19.

INSTRUCTIONS

CO 72 sts, dividing them evenly over 2 circulars
with 36 sts on each ndl. Join, being careful not to
twist cast-on row. Work 15 rnds in k1tbl, p1 ribbing.

LEG
Ndl 1: Work 36 sts in leg pattern 1.
Ndl 2: Work 36 sts in leg pattern 2.
Work a total of 50 rnds in pattern as set (3 x Rnds
1-14 and 1 x Rnds 1-8 in leg pattern 1 and 1 x
Rnds 1-50 of leg pattern 2).
(36+36 sts).

HEEL
Set-up Rnd:
Ndl 1: Work Rnd 9 of leg pattern 1.
Ndl 2: Work Rnd 1 of heel pattern, placing a
marker before the first increase, M1, place
marker.

Rnd 2:
Ndl 1: Work leg pattern 1.
Ndl 2: Work in heel pattern to the 1st marker
without increasing, slip marker, purl to the 2nd
marker, slip marker and work remaining sts in
heel pattern.

Rnd 3:
Ndl 1: Work in leg pattern 1.
Ndl 2: Work in heel pattern to the 1st marker, slip
marker, M1, purl across to next marker, M1, slip
marker and work the rem sts in heel pattern.

Repeat Rnds 2 and 3 another 13 times (29
increases) and then work Rnd 2 (without heel
increases) once more (31 Rnds).
(36+65 sts)

To turn the heel, continue working the sts on ndl 1 in leg pattern 1 and work in short rows over the sts on ndl 2 as follows:

Row 1 (RS): K34, ssk, k1; turn.

Row 2 (WS): Sl 1, p4, p2tog, p1; turn.

Row 3: Sl 1 pwise, knit to 1 st before gap, ssk, k1; turn.

Row 4: Sl 1 pwise, purl to 1 st before gap, p2tog, p1; turn.

Repeat Rows 3-4 another 13 times (35 heel sts remain on ndl 2).

(36+35 sts)

FOOT

Work around. On the first round, slip the first and last sts on ndl 2 (heel) to ndl 1 (instep).

(38+33 sts)

GUSSET

Ndl 1: P1, work 36 sts in leg pattern 1, p1.

Ndl 2: K15, k2tog, k16. (38+32 sts)

Ndl 1: P1, work 36 sts in leg pattern 1, p1.

Ndl 2: K32.

Continue working in pattern as set until foot is 2 in (5 cm) less than total foot length (see Table).

BAND TOE

Knit 1 round over all sts.

Set-up round:

Ndl 1: K4, (k2tog, k5) 4 times, k2tog, k4 (5 sts decreased).

Ndl 2: K32.

(33+32 sts)

Shaping:

Ndl 1: K1, ssk, knit to last 3 sts on ndl and end k2tog, k1.

Ndl 2: Work as for Ndl 1.

Knit 3 rnds and decrease on Rnd 4.

(Knit 2 rnds and dec on Rnd 3) 2 times.

Knit 1 rnd and dec on rnd 2) 4 times

Decrease on each of the next 6 rnds.

FINISHING

Cut yarn and thread end onto tapestry needle. Pull end through remaining 9 sts. Pull tight and then weave in all ends neatly on WS.

Make the second sock the same way.

Shoe size: U.S. (Euro)	6-7 (37)	7-8 (38)	8-9 (39)	9-10 (40)	10-11 (41)	11-12 (42)
Foot length	9 ½ in	9 ½-9 ¾ in	10 in	10 ¼ in	10 ½-10 ¾ in	10 ¾ in
	(24 cm)	(24.5-25 cm)	(25.5 cm)	(26 cm)	(26.5-27 cm)	(27.5 cm)
Sock length heel to toe	7 ½ in	7 ¾-8 in	8 in	8 ¼ in in	8 ½-8 ¾ in	8 ¾ in
	(19 cm)	(19.5-20 cm)	(20.5 cm)	(21 cm)	(21.5-22 cm)	(22.5 cm)

Snow and Ice

Deep in the season, once snow has fallen and the cold has set in for good, a Winter Wonderland surrounds us. The changing winds and the kiss of sunlight mold and melt the snow and ice, leaving behind striking patterns and structures as only nature can create. The wavy pattern on this pair of socks, knit with two colors of yarn, is reminiscent of the undulating surfaces of winter snow drifts.

Snow and Ice

LEVEL OF DIFFICULTY
Intermediate

SIZES
Women's U.S. 5-6, 6-7, 7-8, 8-9, 9-10, 10-11, 11-12 (European 36, 37, 38, 39, 40, 41, 42)

Leg circumference: 8 ¾ -11½ in (22-29 cm)

Foot circumference: 8 -10 ¼ in (20-26 cm)

The length of the sock can be determined by using the respective shoe size.

MATERIALS
Yarn: Fingering (CYCA #1), Trekking Sport (75% wool/25% nylon; 462 yd/100 g), Natural (#1400), 100 g and Trekking Maxima (75% superwash wool/25% nylon; 459 yd/100 g) (#905), 100 g

Needles: 2 circular needles U.S. size 0 or 1.5 (2 or 2.5 mm) or size needed to obtain gauge

Tapestry needle

GAUGE
32 sts and 40 rows in stockinette = 4 x 4 in (10 x 10 cm)

35 sts and 40 rows in two-color stranded knitting = 4 x 4 in (10 x 10 cm)

KNITTING BOOKLET
Charts, p. 20

TECHNIQUES
Twisted cast-on, p. 109

Two-color stranded knitting, pp. 112-113

Right- and left-leaning decreases, p. 109

The "gap" on heel turn, p. 111

RIBBING
*K2 with Natural, p2 with Maxima; rep from * around.

HEEL PATTERN
RS: K1, *Sl 1 pwise, k1; rep from * 15 more times and end with k1WS: K1, p32, k1.

LEG, INSTEP, AND SOLE PATTERNS
See Booklet, p. 20.

INSTRUCTIONS

Twisted Cast-on
With Maxima, CO 72 sts on one circular; turn and knit 1 row.
Attach Natural and knit 2 rows (garter st).
With Maxima, knit 2 rows.

Twisting row
Work 6 sts in rib, holding both working yarns in your left hand, rotate the right needle one full turn; repeat * to * another 11 times.

Slip 36 sts to the second circular and join to work in the round.
Work 10 rnds in rib.
(36+36 sts)

Now work 24 rnds in leg pattern (1 x Rnds 1-16 and then work Rnds 1-8).
Cut Maxima.

HEEL

Slip the first and last sts from ndl 1 to ndl 2 (34+38 sts).

Work in heel pattern over the 34 sts on ndl 1 for 30 rows.

Turn heel:

Row 1 (RS): K19, ssk, k1; turn.

Row 2 (WS): Sl 1, p5, p2tog, p1; turn.

Row 3: Sl 1 pwise, knit until 1 st before the gap, ssk, k1; turn.

Row 4: Sl 1 pwise, purl until 1 st before the gap, p2tog, p1; turn.

Repeat Rows 3-4 another 5 times (20 heel sts remain on ndl 1).

Cut Natural.

GUSSET

Ndl 1: With Natural, pick up and knit 15 sts along right side of heel flap, knit the 20 heel sts, pick up and knit 15 sts along the left side of heel flap.

Ndl 2: K38 with Natural.

Rnd 1:

Ndl 1: Work Rnd 1 of the sole pattern.

Ndl 2: Work Rnd 1 of the Instep pattern.

(50+38 sts)

Rnd 2:

Ndl 1: Work in sole pattern.

Ndl 2: Work in instep pattern.

Continue in pattern to Rnd 26 of the sole pattern and Rnd 10 of the instep. (34+38 sts)

FOOT

Ndl 1: Work Rnd 26 of sole pattern.

Ndl 2: Continue in instep pattern.

Continue in pattern as set until foot is 2 in (5 cm) less than total foot length (see Table).

BAND TOE

Cut Maxima and work the toe in Natural.

Slip the first and last sts of ndl 2 back to ndl 1. (36+36 sts)

Knit 1 rnd over all sts.

Ndl 1: *K4, k2tog*; rep * to * 5 more times.

Ndl 2: Work as for Ndl 1.

Knit 1 rnd.

(30+30 sts)

Shaping:

Ndl 1: K1, ssk, knit to last 3 sts on ndl and end with k2tog, k1.

Ndl 2: Work as for Ndl 1.

Knit 3 rnds and decrease on Rnd 4.

(Knit 2 rnds and dec on Rnd 3) 2 times.

Knit 1 rnd and dec on rnd 2) 3 times

Decrease on each of the next 6 rnds.

FINISHING

Cut yarn and thread end onto tapestry needle. Pull end through remaining 8 sts. Pull tight and then weave in all ends neatly on WS.

Make the second sock the same way.

Shoe size: U.S. (Euro)	5-6 (36)	6-7 (37)	7-8 (38)	8-9 (39)	9-10 (40)	10-11 (41)	11-12 (42)
Foot length	9 ½ in	9 ½ in	9 ½-9 ¾ in	10 in	10 ¼ in	10 ½-10 ¾ in	10 ¾ in
	(23.5 cm)	(24 cm)	(24.5-25 cm)	(25.5 cm)	(26 cm)	(26.5-27 cm)	(27.5 cm)
Sock length heel to toe	7 ¼ in	7 ½ in	7 ¾-8 in	8 in	8 ¼ in in	8 ½-8 ¾ in	8 ¾ in
	(18.5 cm)	(19 cm)	(19.5-20 cm)	(20.5 cm)	(21 cm)	(21.5-22 cm)	(22.5 cm)

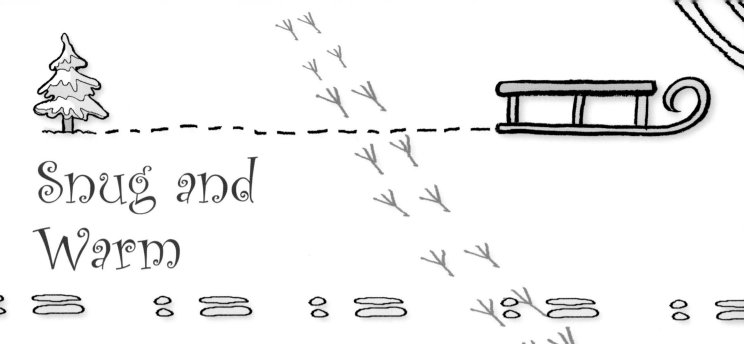

Snug and Warm

When the world has shed its summer attire and chosen a coat of brown, you begin to take notice of the creatures around you as your eyes follow their fresh tracks in the faintest dusting of first snowfall. It is these scurrying paths of busy animals and birds that serve as the inspiration behind this knit pattern. Designed for warm feet with a charming twist, these socks won't lead you astray.

Snug and Warm

LEVEL OF DIFFICULTY
Intermediate

SIZES
Women's U.S. 5-6, 6-7, 7-8, 8-9, 9-10, 10-11, 11-12 (European 36, 37, 38, 39, 40, 41, 42)

Leg circumference: 8-10 ¾ in (20-27 cm)

Foot circumference: 8-9 ¾ in (20-25 cm)

The length of the sock can be determined by using the respective shoe size.

MATERIALS
Yarn: Fingering (CYCA #1), Regia 4-ply Stretch (70% wool/23% nylon/7% polyester; 219 yd/50 g), Military Green (#9996), 100 g

Needles: 2 circular needles U.S. size 0 or 1.5 (2 or 2.5 mm) or size needed to obtain gauge

Cable needle

Tapestry needle

GAUGE
32 sts and 40 rows in stockinette = 4 x 4 in (10 x 10 cm)

36 sts and 40 rows in cable pattern = 4 x 4 in (10 x 10 cm)

KNITTING BOOKLET
Chart, p. 15

TECHNIQUES
Twisted cast-on, p. 109

The "gap" on heel turn, p. 111

RIBBING
*K1tbl, p1; repeat from * around.

LEG AND INSTEP PATTERNS
See Booklet, p. 15.

Rotating the needle point by a full turn:
On the WS of the work, twist the needle down and towards the front and then back around. The cast-on row has now been twisted a full turn.

INSTRUCTIONS

Cast on 72 sts on one of the circular needles and knit 4 rows in garter st.
On the following row, *k6, rotate the right needle; repeat from * across and turn to work back.
Work 36 sts in ribbing, move the next 36 sts to the 2nd circular and work in ribbing; join to work in the round.
Work 14 rnds in ribbing.

LEG
Work 56 rnds in leg pattern (2 x Rnds 1-28), adjusting the cable pattern on the needles as follows:

Rnd 4:
Ndl 1: Work 36 sts of Rnd 4.
Ndl 2: Work 34 sts of Rnd 4; place the last 2 sts onto cable needle and hold in front, k2 from ndl 1.

Rnd 5:
Ndl 1: Work Rnd 5, knit the first 2 sts from cable needle, place the last 2 sts from ndl onto cable ndl and hold in front, and then k2 from ndl 2.
Ndl 2: Knit the first 2 sts of Rnd 5 from cable ndl and knit the last 4 sts on the needle without cabling.

Rnd 22:
Ndl 1: Work 36 sts of Rnd 22.
Ndl 2: Work 34 sts of Rnd 22, place the next 2 sts on cable ndl and hold in back, k2 from ndl 1.

Rnd 23:
Ndl 1: On Rnd 23, knit the 2 sts on cable ndl and place the last 2 sts onto cable ndl and hold in back, k2 from ndl 2.
Ndl 2: On Rnd 23, knit the first 2 sts from cable ndl and knit the last 4 sts on ndl without cabling.

Set-up for Heel:
With ndl 2, slip the first 4 sts of ndl 1 to ndl 2 as

follows: K2, k1tbl, p1.
(32+40 sts)

HEEL

With ndl 1, work the heel back and forth in stockinette over 32 sts and 30 rows. Set sts on ndl 2 aside for instep while you work the heel flap.

Turn heel:

Turn the heel with ndl 1 as follows:

Row 1 (RS): K17, ssk, k1; turn.

Row 2 (WS): Sl 1 purlwise, p3, p2tog, p2; turn.

Row 3: Sl 1 pwise, knit until 1 st before the gap, ssk, k1; turn.

Row 4: Sl 1 pwise, purl until 1 st before the gap, p2tog, p1; turn.

Repeat Rows 3-4 another 5 times (18 heel sts remain on ndl 1).

GUSSET

Rnd 1:

Ndl 1: Knit 18 heel sts and then pick up and knit 15 sts along side of heel flap.

Ndl 2: Work 40 sts in instep pattern.

Rnd 2:

Ndl 1: Pick up and knit 15 sts along side of heel flap, k33.

Ndl 1: Work across in instep pattern.

(48+40 sts).

Rnd 3:

Ndl 1: K1, ssk, knit until 3 sts remain on ndl and end with k2tog, k1.

Ndl 2: Work across in instep pattern.

Rnds 4-5:

Ndl 1: Knit.

Ndl 2: Work across in instep pattern.

Repeat the Rows 3-5 another 7 times (32+40 sts).

FOOT

Ndl 1 (sole): Knit.

Ndl 2 (instep): Continue in instep pattern beginning on Rnd 27.

Continue in pattern until you've worked 28 rnds (Rnds 27-28 and then 1 x Rnds 1-26.

Shaping:

Ndl 1: Knit.

Ndl 2: K2, k1tbl, *p4, place 2 sts onto cable ndl and hold in back, knit the 1st from the working ndl together with the 1st st from the cable ndl and then knit the 2nd st from the working ndl together with the 2nd st from the cable ndl, k4, k1tbl; rep from * another 2 times and end with p1.

(32+34 sts)

Ndl 1: K32.

Ndl 2: K33 and slip the last st to ndl 1.

(33+33 sts)

Continue in pattern as set until foot is 2 in (5 cm) less than total foot length (see Table).

BAND TOE

Shaping

Ndl 1: K1, ssk, knit to last 3 sts on ndl and end with k2tog, k1.

Ndl 2: Work as for ndl 1.

Knit 3 rnds and decrease on Rnd 4.

(Knit 2 rnds and dec on Rnd 3) 2 times.

Knit 1 rnd and dec on rnd 2) 3 times

Decrease on each of the next 7 rnds.

FINISHING

Cut yarn and thread end onto tapestry needle. Pull end through remaining 10 sts. Pull tight and then weave in all ends neatly on WS.

Make the second sock the same way.

Shoe size: U.S. (Euro)	5-6 (36)	6-7 (37)	7-8 (38)	8-9 (39)	9-10 (40)	10-11 (41)	11-12 (42)
Foot length	9 ½ in	9 ½ in	9 ½-9 ¾ in	10 in	10 ¼ in	10 ½-10 ¾ in	10 ¾ in
	(23.5 cm)	(24 cm)	(24.5-25 cm)	(25.5 cm)	(26 cm)	(26.5-27 cm)	(27.5 cm)
Sock length heel to toe	7 ¼ in	7 ½ in	7 ¾-8 in	8 in	8 ¼ in in	8 ½-8 ¾ in	8 ¾ in
	(18.5 cm)	(19 cm)	(19.5-20 cm)	(20.5 cm)	(21 cm)	(21.5-22 cm)	(22.5 cm)

Basics & Knitting Techniques

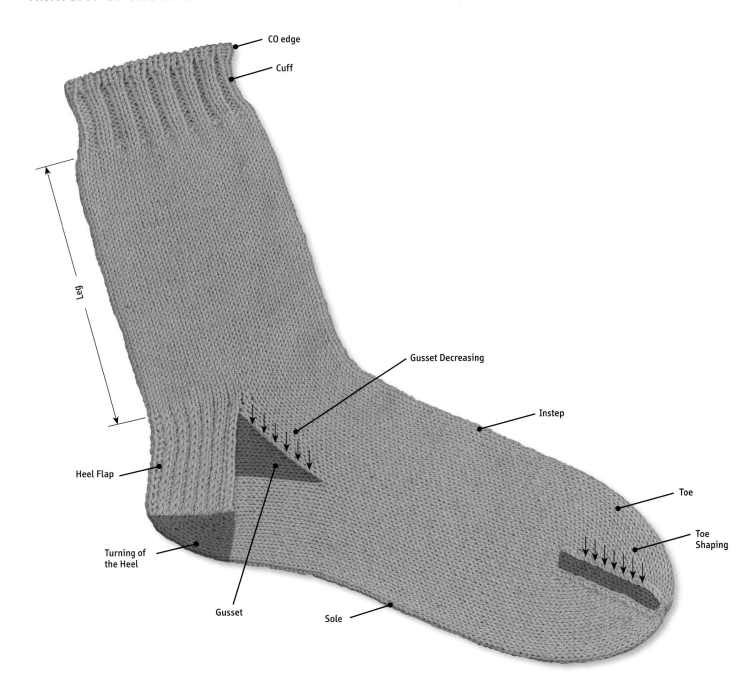

CO edge

Cuff

Leg

Gusset Decreasing

Instep

Heel Flap

Toe

Turning of
the Heel

Toe
Shaping

Gusset

Sole

From the cast on edge, stitches are divided among needles which are numbered clockwise (usually beginning at the back of the heel). The instructions provide you with the number of stitches to put on each needle, for example (15, 16, 17, 18 sts) means to put 15 stitches on needle one, 16 sts, on needle two, 17 sts on needle three, and 18 sts on needle four.

The heel is most often knit across the sts on needles one and four so that the row change is at the back of the sock and under the foot. Sometimes the pattern is such that it is simpler to have the row change at the side of the sock and the heel worked on a different pair of needles. However, depending on the pattern, or whether you are knitting on two circular needles, stitch distribution can vary. These differences will be stated clearly in the directions.

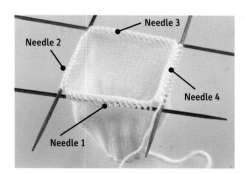

Needle 3
Needle 2
Needle 4
Needle 1

When knitting socks, the stitches are usually distributed as evenly as possible among the four double points, or the two circulars.

Sometimes it's easier to knit a pattern if the entire pattern repeat is on one needle. Or, sometimes it is easier to center an instep pattern by rearranging the stitch distribution, even if the stitch count on the needles is uneven.

Such uneven stitch distributions make it possible to achieve "travelling stitches" by slipping stitches from one needle to another without knitting them.

Should it become necessary to alter the stitch distribution, it will be clearly stated in the directions.

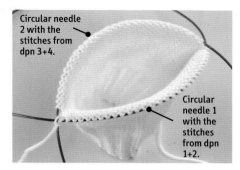

Circular needle 2 with the stitches from dpn 3+4.

Circular needle 1 with the stitches from dpn 1+2.

Knitting in the round on two circular needles is a particularly good technique if you are working on a pattern with a large repeat, especially in two-color knitting. You'll want to avoid the "joint" which sometimes results between two double pointed needles in the middle of your pattern. The stitches which are normally on needles 1 and 2 should be placed on the first circular needle and the stitches normally found on needles 3 and 4 should be placed on the second circular needle. Keep this "formula" in mind for easy conversion from double points to circular needles.

When knitting with two circular needles, be careful that you never have more than half the stitch count on the straight part of the needle at one time. The other half of the stitches should be "on hold" on the cable.

LIFTED BAR INCREASE (M1)

With the right-hand needle, from behind, pick up the horizontal bar between two stitches as shown. Insert the left-hand needle into the front of the lifted stitch and knit.

RIGHT-LEANING INCREASE FROM ROW BELOW

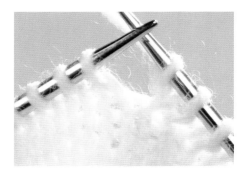

With the left-hand needle, from behind, pick up the purl bump beneath the stitch just worked as shown. Knit the stitch.

LEFT-LEANING INCREASE FROM ROW BELOW

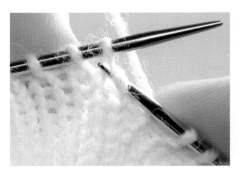

With the right-hand needle, from behind, pick up the purl bump of the next stitch from the row below and knit through back loop. Work next stitch in pattern.

RIGHT AND LEFT-LEANING DECREASES

When you knit two stitches together, they will lean to the right or the left, depending on which stitch is lying on top. These decreases are especially important if you are knitting a complex lace pattern, a gusset after the heel or symmetric toe band.

RIGHT-LEANING

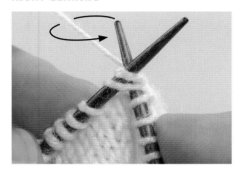

Knit two stitches together as one (k2tog).

LEFT-LEANING

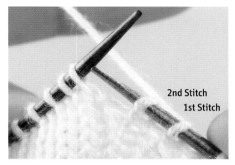

2nd Stitch
1st Stitch

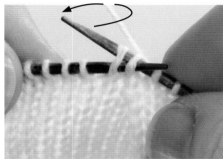

Slip the next two stitches separately onto the right hand needle, as if to knit. Slip the left-hand needle into the front of the slipped stitches and knit the two together (ssk).

GARTER STITCH TWISTED CUFF

For a twisted cuff in garter stitch, start by knitting back and forth for the designated number of rows.

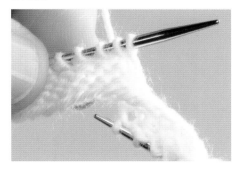

MAKE ONE TWIST

Hold the working yarn securely with the left hand. Once you have worked the correct number of stitches, take the tip of the right needle around the back of the work and come forward from underneath. Return to the original spot. The cast on edge has now been twisted once.

SHORT ROWS WITH WRAPPED STITCHES

Short rows are worked by knitting an incomplete row and then turning the work. In order to avoid a hole at the turn, there is a special way to work the stitch which acts as the transition to the rest of the knitting. You'll end up with smooth transitions when knitting short rows (with either toes or heels) if you use wrapped stitches.

WRAP AND TURN (RS)

Hold yarn in back. With right-hand needle, slip the next stitch purlwise, bring yarn to the front between the needles. Slip the stitch back to the left-hand needle and turn work. Bring yarn to front and begin the new row.

WRAP AND TURN (WS)

Hold the yarn in front. With right-hand needle, slip the next stitch purlwise, take yarn to the back. Slip the stitch back to the left-hand needle and turn work. Take yarn to the back and begin the new row.

WORKING WRAPPED STITCHES

When working heels and toe up socks with short rows, most stitches only need to wrapped once, but some twice.

From the right side, as if to knit, place needle tip under the "wrap(s)" and pull it up onto the left-hand needle next to the stitch it was wrapped around. Knit them together.

WORKING WRAPPED STITCHES (WS)

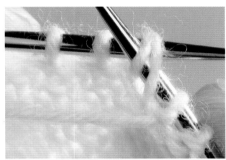

From the wrong side, as if to purl, place needle tip under the "wrap(s)" and pull it up onto the left-hand needle next to the stitch it was wrapped around. Purl them together.

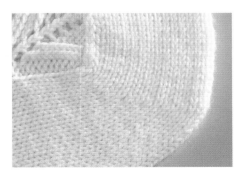

THE "GAP" ON HEEL TURN

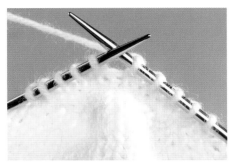

When turning the heel, in each round, the last stitch of the middle section is knit together with the first stitch of the side section. As you continue to work back and forth, a shortened row is created and the heel is turned. At the turning point is a little triangle between the stitches that is known as the heel gusset.

TWO-COLOR STRANDED KNITTING

These patterns are knit with at least two colors per row, a background color and a contrast color. As a rule they are knit in stockinette stitch and motifs are charted.

While you are knitting with one color, the other is floating across the back of the work. The more stitches there are to be knit in a given color, the longer the floats. The floats shouldn't exceed eight to ten stitches when working with 4-ply sock yarn and a US needle size of 1-3 (2.25-3.25mm).

TRAPPING THE FLOATS

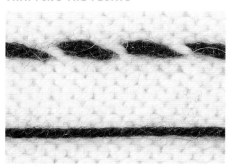

There is a risk of getting snagged when putting on or taking off a sweater with floats. To prevent this, catch the float about midway through so that it is snug against the fabric. When trapping the float, prevent its showing through by trapping the yarn behind a stitch of a less contrasting color.

LENGTH OF FLOATS

For a smooth consistent fabric, it is important that the length of the float be as even as possible.

To prevent a float that is too short which causes puckering, spread out the sts on the right-hand needle. Press your right index finger on the working yarn so that when knitting, the float will be the right length.

CHANGING NEEDLES

The next big challenge is changing needles. The most helpful technique is to spread the sts as wide as they will be when the sock is on the foot. Hold the yarn near the needle. After knitting the first stitch in the new color, line up the previous needle and the new needle and determine the float length.

Beginners often find stranded knitting easier on two circular needles. You only have half the difficult needle changes to manage and the flexible cable of the circular needle makes it easier to find places where floats might be too tight.

How you choose to hold your yarn is a matter of personal preference. Being relaxed and creating a nice smooth fabric are more important than speed. The best thing to do is experiment with the suggested methods and figure out what works best for you.

To hold both strands in the left hand, lay them both over the left index finger. You might even wrap them around your pinky to help with tension. When one color is used more often than the other, it becomes more tightly wrapped around your finger. This method of holding the yarn allows you to quickly adjust the length of both strands and return to your customary hold while knitting. One disadvantage of this method for holding yarn is that both strands are held to the side along with the working needle and can become easily twisted.

A variation on both strands in the left hand is to lay the first strand, as usual, from back to front over the left index finger, then lay the second strand from front to back. Then wrap both strands together one more time around the left pinky. This grasp prevents the twisting of the yarn considerably, but it is more difficult to keep both strands the same length.

To knit with one strand in each hand, one strand of each color lays over each index finger. Each strand must be allowed to run through the fingers at a different rate in order to maintain the same length. Yarns hardly ever get tangled using this method and it is no problem to use the yarns up at different rates. This grasp requires a little practice and is suitable for more experienced knitters.

Lastly, the easiest way to knit with two colors is to carry one yarn at a time. Lay the working strand over the left index finger (Continental method) or over the right index finger (English style). The other strand hangs off the back. To change colors, drop the first strand and pick up the second strand accordingly. The tension is easiest to manage with this method and even beginners are quick to experience success. It is easy to trap a float and as you are manually wrapping the yarns around one another, it is easy to prevent tangles.

GAUGE

Stranded knitting fabric is always tighter than stockinette fabric. This means that the sock will need more stitches to achieve the same circumference. Stranded knitting is also somewhat less elastic, so there should be a little extra width built into the sock as well. The floats running through the inside of the sock help make it thicker and warmer than a solid color sock knit from the same yarn.

Be sure to block stranded knitting when complete, or at least dampen and stretch gently into desired shape. It will become more even in appearance.

This type of sock toe is both comfortable and elegant. It is most easily knit with two circular needles. The trick is to cast stitches on to a circular needle and then slide the stitches down to the flexible cable. The cable is thinner and more flexible than the metal needle. You can then use a second circular needle to pick up and knit from the underside of the cast on stitches.

With the first circular, cast on the number of stitches plus one additional stitch required for the blunt toe. Work a long tail cast on with the tail yarn over the index finger and the working yarn over the thumb. Then later you can let the extra stitch drop.

Slide the stitches on to the flexible part of the needle.

Turn work so that both cast on strands are on the right side. Rotate the work so that the cast on edge is now sitting on top of the needle.
With the second circular needle, insert the tip into the cast on edge between two stitches and knit up one stitch.
You'll end up with one more stitch on the first needle than on the second needle.

With the first needle, knit to the last stitch. Let the last stitch fall and secure it with the tail yarn.

The completed toe-up tip.

CROCHETED BOBBLE

The following stitch is worked with a crochet hook inserted through the knit stitch.
*Ch 1, yarn around hook; rep from * 2 more times = 6 loops around hook.

Pull the last loop through the other 5 loops. Holding the crochet hook with bobble below the knitting needle, insert hook through the loop of the stitch below the next st on needle. Bring the loop through the last crocheted loop to secure the bobble and then slide the new st to the right needle.

PICOT CROCHET EDGING

Slip the last st onto the crochet hook and work the picot edging along bind-off row:
*Ch 3, sl st into first st of chain, skip 2 sts on bind-off row, sc into next st; rep from * around. Cut yarn, thread end onto tapestry needle, and pull end through last st. Weave in ends neatly on WS.

KNOTTED EDGING

First, knit the specified number of strips. They will be lined up side by side on the circular needle with st st on the right side facing you.

KNOT THE FIRST TWO STRIPS:

Place the cast on stitches of the second strip onto an extra needle and rotate once clockwise. Then knit together one st of the first strip together with one cast on st of the second strip. The stitches on both needles should present stockinette stitch on the right side of the fabric.

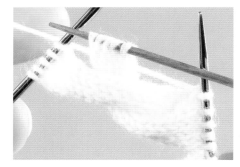

Bring the stitches from the first strip around the second, from back to front. Then, knit each st of the second strip together with each cast on edge stitch of the first stitch. Again, be sure that when you knit the pieces together, both stockinette stitch sides present as the right sides.

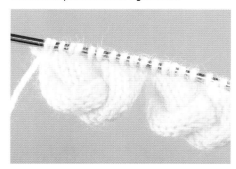

Continue working in this way, knotting two strips as you go. Distribute the stitches of the cuff evenly around the needle.

KNITTING WITH BEADS

The 2.6 mm beads are especially well-suited for knitting socks with 4-ply yarn. Craft and bead shops offer many different colors and finishes.

STRINGING BEADS

Before casting on, you'll need to string the beads onto the working yarn.

It is simplest to use a sewing needle: Cut a 12-16" piece of strong sewing thread. Fold it in half and thread it through the sewing needle. Pull about 8" of yarn through the loop. With the help of the sewing needle, all the beads can be slid onto the sock yarn. To count the beads, it is helpful to pick up 5 at a time and slide them up the yarn in blocks of 50. Once all beads are threaded, they'll need to be slid about 3 yds further up the yarn. First cast on, and follow instruction as given. Pull the beads up into your knitting, or slide them further toward the ball as needed.

KNITTING BEADS

On the marked squares of the chart, insert ndl as if to knit, pull a bead up close to the needle and as you knit the stitch, pull the bead through too. The bead should sit on the right leg of the stitch.

KNITTING TWISTED BEAD STITCHES

The simplest way to put beads into knitting is with a twisted stitch. The stitch which contains a bead is knit as a twisted stitch in the following row or round and the bead is fixed in its position. Knitting beads into twisted stitches is typically used when you want to use a single row of beads in your design.

In the following row or rnd, knit every stitch as a twisted stitch. This rotates both legs of the stitch so that the beads cannot slip. Be aware while knitting that the bead must sit on the right leg of the stitch.

BEAD STITCHES IN STOCKINETTE STITCH

The stitches seem more even when the beads are knit into stockinette stitches. You have to watch closely because a bead can slip easily from the right to left leg of a stitch which changes the appearance of the pattern. Knitting beads in stockinette stitch fabric is well-suited for knitting an entire pattern. When a bead is in place and you are on the next row, work it as a knit stitch regardless of whether you'll be knitting another bead in or not.

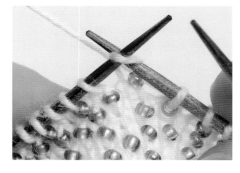

In order to knit the bead when it is not on the right leg of the stitch, it is helpful to slip the bead stitch as if to knit, then with the left needle, from left to right, insert needle and knit. This allows you to control the position of the bead more easily.

Bead knitting in stockinette stitch should not be too loose. If it is, you may find that after the laundry, you beads have migrated to the inside of your sock.

GAUGE

Save yourself time and aggravation by knitting a gauge swatch before you begin your project! Many patterns vary significantly in their gauge from stockinette stitch. So be sure to complete your gauge swatch so that your sock fits well. If necessary, you can vary the needle size to obtain the correct gauge.

Before measuring, dampen the fabric, but no ironing!

If there are too many stitches in the 4x4 in swatch, then the knitting was too tight, or the floats across the back of the sweater were pulled too tightly. In this case, too much elasticity is lost and the sock will feel too tight. Choose a .25 to .5mm larger needle for the next swatch.

If there are too few stitches in the 4x4 in swatch, the knitting was too loose and the sock measurements too large. These socks will tend to fall down and if they are worked in two-color knitting, the contrast color will show through when you wear them. Choose a .25 to .5mm smaller needle for the next swatch.

MEASURING SOCK LENGTH

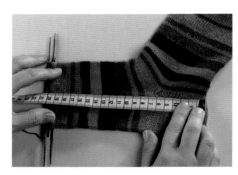

Lay your sock out flat on a table . Use a measuring tape to measure from the outermost edge of the heel to your last knit round. Begin the heel when the length of your sock corresponds to the desired length given in the chart.

BIND OFF LOOSELY

Knit 2, slip stitches back on the left-hand needle and knit together through back loops.
*Knit 1, slip stitches back on the left-hand needle and knit together through back loops, repeat from *. Continue until all stitches have been worked and only one remains.

WEAVING IN ENDS

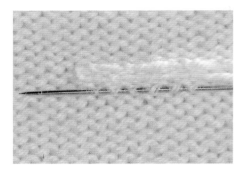

Weaving in the ends on socks takes more care because there are no edge stitches or seams at your disposal to pull yarn through.

It is easy to hide ends in the cast on edge as well as the toe.

You must be careful with ends in the middle of your sock, as with stranded knitting in general. A sharp embroidery needle makes it possible to pull ends through a single strand on the inside of the sock.

The floats are also a good place to weave in the ends of stranded knitting.

ABBREVIATIONS

BO	bind off
ch	chain
cm	centimeter(s)
CO	cast on
dpn	double-pointed needle(s)
in	inch(es)
inc	increase
g	gram(s)
k	knit
k2tog	knit 2 together
kwise	knitwise (insert needle into st as if to knit)
m	meter(s)
mm	millmeter(s)
M1	make 1 (increase by lifting strand between two sts and knit into back loop)
ndl(s)	needle(s)
p	purl
p2tog	purl 2 together

psso	pass slipped st over
pwise	purlwise (insert needle into st as if to purl, holding yarn in back of work unless otherwise noted)
rem	remain(s, -ing)
rep	repeat(s)
rnd	round(s)
RS	right side
sc	single crochet
sl	slip
ssk	sl 1 knitwise, sl 1 knitwise, insert left needle into front loops and knit together)
st(s)	stitch(es)
St st	stockinette stitch
tbl	through back loop(s)
tog	together
w&t	wrap and turn
WS	wrong side

STEPHANIE VAN DER LINDEN

Since my early childhood, I have been knitting, crocheting, embroidering and sewing with great enthusiasm. I studied chemistry and civil engineering and later worked in the field of civil engineering. This probably explains my fascination with the structure of knit and purl stitches. Excited by the look and feel of various textiles and fiber, I began designing at an early age. The juxtaposition of color, form, and symmetry is a challenge when designing unusual and detail-rich patterns. I create designs for German and international magazines, publishers and yarn manufacturers. I also correspond with knitters and sock enthusiasts from around the world – it is wonderful to see what magic others create with my patterns!

MANY HEARTFELT THANKS to my husband Johannes and my daughters Lioba, Dorothea, and Silja for their great patience and understanding!
MANY HEARTFELT THANKS to Melitta Gaertner and Carola Aichinger for knitting the samples.
MANY HEARTFELT THANKS to Mariann Andersen: Many thanks for helping me so quickly!

YARN SUPPLIERS

Westminster Fibers
165 Ledge Street
Nashua, NH 03060
800-445-9276
www.westminsterfibers.com

Webs—America's Yarn Store
75 Service Center Road
Northampton, MA 01060
800-367-9327
www.yarn.com
customerservice@yarn.com

For more information on selecting or substituting yarn contact your local yarn shop or an online store, they are familiar with all types of yarns and would be happy to help you. Additionally, the online knitting community at Ravelry.com has forums where you can post questions about specific yarns. Yarns come and go so quickly these days and there are so many beautiful yarns available.